CROSS THIS BRIDGE AT A WALK

by Jared Carter

books

Cross this Bridge at a Walk
Les Barricades Mystérieuses
After the Rain
Work, for the Night Is Coming

chapbooks

Reading the Tarot
Blues Project
Situation Normal
The Shriving
Millennial Harbinger
Pincushion's Strawberry
Fugue State
Early Warning

Cross this Bridge at a Walk

Jared Carter

WIND PUBLICATIONS
2006

International Standard Book Number 1893239462
Library of Congress Control Number 2005931649

First edition

Front cover photo by Jared Carter — Interior of the Medora Covered Bridge, built in 1875 by Joseph J. Daniels. The bridge, located east of the town of Medora in Jackson County, Indiana, crosses the east fork of the White River. Now preserved at an off-road site, it is the last surviving triple-span bridge in the state. At a length of 458 feet, or 139.6 meters—the equivalent of one and one-half football fields—it is also the longest covered bridge still standing in the United States.

Back cover photo by Diane Carter — In the keep of the Castelo de Almourol, Portugal, summer of 2005.

for Misch and John Ertel

Contents

It is said children still have a sense of wonder, later one becomes blunted. — Nonsense. A child takes things for granted, and most people get no further; only an *old* person, who *thinks*, is aware of the wondrous.

Victor Klemperer, *I Will Bear Witness*

Cross this Bridge at a Walk

Raccoon Grove

> Let the mighty mounds
> That overlook the rivers, or that rise
> In the dim forest crowded with old oaks,
> Answer.
>
>> William Cullen Bryant
>> "The Prairies"

To go, if there is time, to look at what
the land holds — some feature of their world
they wish to share, whether it be host
or stranger who comes up after the reading
and says "If you've time tomorrow morning,
there's something that might interest you."
I find a way to meet them, to go see.

Every place has its secrets, its holes
and entryways into the earth, its shafts
abandoned and still burning underground,
its desert reaches: natural bridges spaced
through an entrenched meander; salt marsh
and bayou darkened by canvasback rising;
ridges stripped and gashed and left barren.

Always they want to visit wild places:
sail the catamaran across to Michigan's
archipelago, so far out the curvature
of earth hides everything but water and sky;
canoe down a spring-fed river in the Ozarks
through long tunnels of sycamores arching
smooth and white above their own reflections.

"I'm a landscape gardener," this man said,
after we had talked about the college
and all the good things it was doing.

3

"When the workshop's over tomorrow,
there's a place I'd like to take you to.
It's called Raccoon Grove. It's right
on the edge of where the prairie begins."

The next day we drove through the town.
"Germans built it," he explained, pointing
at the scroll-saw porches. "A station
on the Illinois Central. They used to raise
horses here. There was a lot of trading."
We stopped at a cemetery south of town:
all the old names were in black letter.

"My brother and I come here once a year,
in the winter, after the first snowfall.
We camp out, up there, along that ridge,
the way we used to do, years ago.
He's an architect now. We stay up
most of the night and talk. Nurse the fire.
Try to remember what we heard back then.

"Camped in Raccoon Grove every summer,
too, in those days. An old man told us
how he found a grave once, surrounded
by logs, when he was a boy. It was
an Indian princess's grave, he said,
with four big cedar logs around it.
We looked, but we never found anything.

"In the spring, after the first plowing,
we used to wait for a rain, then start
walking out across all this flat land.
Imagine yourself a thousand years ago
looking for a place to spend the night.
Maybe over there. Go that way, even now,
poke around, you'd find points and flints."

We parked and started into the grove.
It was all red oak and shagbark hickory
and no sound where we stepped, the leaves
so thick, the creek so still. A warm day
in late March, the equinox, too early
for wildflowers, leaves beginning to show,
stalks of unfolded fern springing up.

We followed the creek upstream. I saw
no litter anywhere, no sign of waste.
"It's not a park," he said. "The city
owns it. Everybody knows it's here.
Just a place to come and walk sometimes,
maybe camp for the night. Each of us
has old reasons for caring about it."

We crossed over and came to a high place
of bare earth and roots showing, stones
and sections of log ringing a fire pit.
It seemed a good place to rest. We sat
listening to the wind make the trees creak.
"The things you said last night," he began,
"or spoke, in your poems, about the earth — "

He fell silent for a moment. "I've been
all over this country. Alaska. Texas.
Lived with an uncle in Canada. Hitch-hiked
around Europe." I nodded. I'd done that too.
"Spent a lot of time in southwest England
and Wales, looking at those big stones."
I nodded again. I hadn't been there yet.

"Last night you talked about the mounds —
there," he said, pointing south, toward
the Wabash and the Ohio. "The old ones,
bordering the rivers, that go back a long way.

You had a grant to look at things like that."
"People are curious," I said. "They hope
someone might tell them what it means."

"And can you?" "No. Only that we're all
still looking, still trying to understand.
When there's time, I go out to those places,
those covered bridges, those brick sidewalks
hidden in the grass, that don't lead anywhere.
I read the old writers, too, the forgotten ones,
those who wrote about how that world looked.

"It doesn't matter if they're not remembered.
They saw the same things then that we see now.
It doesn't change that much — not the trees,
not the animals, not the sound of the birds.
You can walk out onto one of those mounds
all by yourself, in that stillness, and know
it's unchanged. Same river down there, flowing."

It was time to go. We walked toward the car.
"I don't read much," he said. "I know green things.
Once in a while, out like this, I'll see trees
that look as though someone had planted them
in a straight line. When an old tree leans,
sometimes it will sucker out along one side.
When it finally goes down, all those branches

become new trees, standing in a row, growing
out of the old one. You can read them
like an arrow blazed there, an inscription
for those who come after." "For those,"
I said, "who take the time to look, who want
to see." "Yes." We drove back to town.
The sun was still high when we shook hands.

Exhumation

By 1835 the Shaker communities had grown and prospered —
at twelve locations in New England and, farther west,
on the frontier, at six villages in Ohio and Kentucky.
The earliest of these settlements, near the present city
of Albany, was called Watervliet. When the visionary,
Ann Lee, joined her followers there in early 1776,
two years after emigrating from Manchester, England,
she found a wilderness. *Trees had to be felled,*   ANDREWS
swamps drained, land tilled, and buildings erected.
During the next half century that same wilderness
would become one of the most important settlements
of the Shakers — the United Society of Believers
in Christ's Second Appearing.

By the spring of 1835
Watervliet was a prosperous, self-sustaining village
of three hundred Believers. Consecrating "hands to work,
hearts to God," members led celibate, cloistered lives,
dealing only indirectly with the outside world. Many
who had been taken in as orphans knew no other way
of life, and were content.

A common burying ground
had been established across the road and to the west
of the Church Family dwelling house. To this place,
in that year, the elders decided to move the remains
of Mother Ann Lee, founder of the Society, along with
her brother William, and a man named William Bigsby.
Fifty years earlier, during the time of persecution
and trouble, their bodies had been buried in a plot
east of the village. In those days the settlement
was sometimes called Niskayuna, after the Indians
who lived nearby.

In 1782 the colonies were at war.
Shakers in New England commonly met and worshipped
in private homes. Because their leaders had come
from England, because of the exuberant ways in which
they danced and sang, they were rumored to be spies,
royalists, traitors, lewd persons who cavorted naked
and trafficked in witchcraft.

                    In the town of Petersham,
Massachusetts, as the Shakers held evening worship
in the home of David Hammond, men bearing torches
battered down the doors and burst into the room.
Hammond and his wife and small child were knocked down,   ANDREWS
and Elder James [Whittaker] was felled to the floor
and left for dead. Rummaging through the house
the mob found Ann Lee in a bedroom and *immediately*
seized her by the feet, and inhumanly dragged her,
feet foremost, out of the house, and threw her
into a sleigh, with as little ceremony as they would
the dead carcase of a beast, and drove off, committing
at the same time, acts of inhumanity and indecency
which even savages would be ashamed of . . . She lost
her cap and handkerchief, and otherwise had her clothes
torn in a shameful manner. Their pretence was to find out
whether she was a woman or not.

                    Although angry mobs
continued to pursue them, *the early summer of 1782*   ANDREWS
found Mother Ann, Father James, and other leaders
preaching at Harvard, Shirley, Still River, Bolton,
and Woburn.

                    In August a group of patriots led
by Captain Phineas Farnworth of the local militia
assembled to drive the Shakers living near Bolton
toward the town of Lancaster, seven miles away.
Men mounted on horses flogged the Shaker company.
It was *one continued scene of cruelty and abuse:*   ANDREWS
whipping with horsewhips, pounding, beating and

bruising with clubs, collaring, pushing off from
bridges, into the water and mud. . . . The leaders
particularly hoped to find English-born Shakers
and discovered one in William Shepherd.

They formed
a ring, and sent one of the mob into the bushes,
to cut sticks for the purpose. He soon returned
with his arms full, and distributed them among
the company. . . each one was appointed to give him
a certain number of strokes.

He was ordered   HORGAN
to strip to the waist, and, as he took off his coat
and jacket, he said to the brethren, "Be of good cheer;
for it is your Heavenly Father's good pleasure
to give you the Kingdom." As Shepherd's reward
for this profession of faith, Isaiah Whitney
administered several lashes with his horsewhip.
Eleazer Rand leaped on Shepherd's back to protect him.
The incensed mob proceeded to flail away at both
of them. A Bolton man named Priest seized Rand,
beat him, and hurled him against a stone wall
in a vain attempt to silence outcries of prayer.
A Harvard citizen, William Morey, protested,
but Captain Farnworth punched him in the face
with such force that he knocked out several teeth.
Morey, with blood streaming from his mouth, continued
to protest. . . . Eleazer Rand was struck by a club,
suffering a broken arm.

Straggling back to Harvard,
the Shakers were again accosted; Abijah Worster
was tied to a tree at the house of Captain Pollard.
Jonathan Houghton laid on the first ten strokes,   HORGAN
but the infamous sport was interrupted when
a respected member of the community, James Haskell,
rode by and rebuked the mob. Haskell tore off
his coat and shrieked, "Here, here, if there are

9

any more stripes to be taken let me take the rest."
Worster was released.

THREE   On the 9th of May, 1835,
before the bodies of the founders could be moved,
it was first necessary to move still another grave.
That morning, representatives of the Ministry set out
for the common burying ground, where they undertook
to reposition the grave of Mother Lucy Wright,
who became head of the Shaker sisterhood in 1787,
after the death of James Whittaker. In the decades
to follow, Lucy Wright would become the Society's
chief spiritual leader, second in importance
only to Mother Ann herself.

                  While still a young woman,
come from Pittsfield to a Shaker meeting at Harvard,
Lucy Wright had been drawn by the *singing, dancing,*   HORGAN
leaping, shouting, clapping of hands, and other . . .
exercises as they were led into by the spirit.
That same night a mob of four hundred surrounded
the house and demanded Ann Lee be given to them.
Lucy Wright was pushed down a flight of stairs
but managed to escape and warn others.

                        Her memory
was greatly esteemed by those about to uncover
her grave now, half a century later. A survey
of the plot indicated that her remains should be
moved *directly to the South, nearly the width*   BUCKINGHAM
of the coffin, bringing it in range with . . . graves
immediately south of where she was formerly lain.

The coffin was found to be very much decayed . . .
but the bodily appearance of the deceased,
who had been therein deterred for the space
of fourteen years and three months . . . retained

10

much of its former shape. . . . Her features
were quite extinct. . . . two teeth. . . .
found loose . . . were reserved as a memorial;
together with a small lock of hair, which still
retained its natural color and beauty; her hair pin,
that was supposed to have been made of whalebone;
and the silken cord that bound her hair.

Two days later
the Ministry, and a goodly number of leading characters
from the different families throughout the Society,
together with a number of the common members, convened
for the purpose of digging up the remains of Mother Ann,
Father William, and William Bigsby.

FOUR   On June 1, 1783,
while the revolution continued, the Shakers were driven
from Harvard to Shirley. The mob singled out William Lee
and James Whittaker, who were known to be English Shakers.
Father James was again scourged "till his back was all   HORGAN
in a gore of blood and the flesh bruised to a jelly."
A neighbor woman, Bethia Willard, tried to protect
Whittaker. She was severely beaten, receiving wounds
which left her scarred for life.

Before leaving England
James Whittaker had a vision of the church of Christ   ANDREWS
in America, which was like a large tree whose leaves
"shone with such brightness, as made it appear
like a burning torch."

Upon the deaths of the Lees,
Whittaker succeeded to the leadership of the Society.
For the next three years he devoted all his energies
to preaching, building meeting houses, and traveling
among the New England settlements. Then *his strength*
began to fail. Only thirty-six, he died in 1787.
A Shaker convert from Connecticut, Joseph Meacham,
became the new "father." To lead the Shaker sisters,
Lucy Wright stepped forward.

Earlier, in the summer
of 1784, William Bigsby, then twenty-two years old
and in *feeble health*, journeyed to Niskayuna,   BUCKINGHAM
anxious to arrive at the latter place, that he might
see and deliver himself to Mother Ann. Whatever
took place between them is not known.
                                        A witness
to those last days, Thankful Barce, wrote of her visit: ANDREWS
"When I arrived, Mother Ann met me at the door. . . .
She sat down in a chair, and I sat down by her side.
Her eyes were shut, and it appeared that her sense
was withdrawn from the things of time. She sung
very melodiously, and appeared very beautiful. . . .
at every touch of her hand, I instantly felt
the power of God run through my whole body. . . . "

William Bigsby died sometime during the autumn
of 1784 and was buried alongside the founders,
"Mother and Father." Ann Lee and her brother William
succumbed to injuries and "a general weariness."

FIVE   On that May morning in 1835, *the business proceeded*   BUCKINGHAM
       in perfect Union, order, and regularity (yet without
       any particular formal ceremony) and by diligent use
       of shovels, alternately handed from one to another,
       the depth of six feet was soon gained. . . .

       Very soon was discovered the skull bone of Mother Ann,
       and after some minutes of diligent and careful searching,
       the bones were principally, if not all, found . . .
       and conveyed above ground on a board previously
       prepared for that purpose. . . .
                            The relics of Father
       were soon found and on another board conveyed above,
       . . . . And now to accomplish the intended business
       of the day, the man previously mentioned by the name
       of William Bigsby . . . was also found. . . .

The boards containing the relics were carried
by nine persons (three to each board) to the village,
. . . to be enclosed in coffins, ready for interment
. . . the following day.
                              As many were desirous
of seeing the relics of Mother and Father, there was
general liberty given; consequently, it became
a prevalent feeling and all, or nearly all, both old
and young, male and female throughout the Society,
came to be eye-witness of the scene.
                                   The boards
were conveyed to the meeting house and arranged
on trestles, while the carpenters and their assistants
brought in the new coffins.
                         The Watervliet meeting house
is a wide, high-ceilinged room with wooden pegs fixed
along the walls, on which portable candle-holders,
made by hand from strips of butternut, each holding
two wax candles, may be hung.
                         Among those Shakers
assembling for a last farewell were certain elders
now between their seventieth and eightieth years,
men and women who had helped found the Society
at the beginning, in the first days — who had left
their homes while still quite young and hopeful,
who had forsaken all else, in some instances even
their own spouses, who had given up what little
they possessed, electing to hold worldly goods
in common with their new brothers and sisters.

They had been Believers now for half a century.
They had traveled for days or weeks, from many parts
of New England and farther west, to sojourn there.
Some of them *had formerly been acquainted with*   BUCKINGHAM

13

Mother & Father, in the days of their ministration,
and had been witnesses of the persecution they suffered
on account of their religion.
                      On the skull bones
was plainly to be seen, fractures of no small magnitude
occasioned by blows and cruel treatment inflicted
upon them by persecuting mobs & on account of their
religious faith and peculiar mode of worship.

There is no contemporary account, no list of names
of members who may have come to the meeting house
on that particular evening. After the younger Shakers
had gone on about their tasks — it was late spring,
time for working in the gardens — four or five elders
may have continued to keep vigil, sitting quietly
on wooden benches which would have been moved out
from the walls. There is no way of knowing how long
they may have remained, past nightfall.
                              The next day,
the necessary graves having been dug, the coffins
were conveyed by wagon to the common burying ground.
And it was thought proper to accomplish or terminate   BUCKINGHAM
the business in like manner, it had thus far proceeded
without much procession or formal ceremony; therefore
nine members were appointed to inter the bones of
the deceased, and accomplish the removal of the relics
of Mother Ann, Father William, and William Bigsby.

SIX   The original brick dormitories of the Church Family
and the South Family are still standing. Today
they house a senior citizen's retirement home
operated by the State of New York. Surrounding lands
once farmed by the Shakers have been covered over
by a country club and golf course, a baseball stadium
with asphalt parking lots, and the concrete runways
of the Albany Airport. Beyond are the shopping malls
and Interstate Highway 87.

The common burying ground
is surrounded on four sides by large maple trees.
There are sixteen rows of gravestones; each row is
thirty-five stones wide. All face west. Lucy Wright,
Ann Lee, and William Lee are buried side by side.

Next to the cemetery, an orchard originally laid out
by the Shakers still contains a few apple trees.
These may have been tended by the last Shakers
to reside at Watervliet, who were removed in 1938.
Preservationists plan to repopulate the grove
with the kinds of trees originally planted there —
a type of apple called the "Duchess of Oldenburg,"
for example. They especially hope to re-establish
a variety of winter apple favored by the Shakers
for making pies. It is, due to its coarse skin
and russet color, no longer sold commercially,
and mostly forgotten.

SEVEN   In the book of Revelation   ANDREWS
there are "two witnesses" to the ultimate mysteries.
They speak of "a woman clothed with the sun," a woman
who "fled into the wilderness, where she hath a place
prepared of God. . . ."

Sources

ANDREWS, Edward Deming. *The People Called Shakers*. New York: Dover, 1963.

BUCKINGHAM. Copy of a Letter to Eldress Ruth Langdon: 1835. Photocopy of typescript courtesy of the Shaker Library, Sabbathday Lake.

HORGAN, Edward R. *The Shaker Holy Land: A Community Portrait*. Harvard, Massachusetts: The Harvard Common Press, 1982

Covered Bridge

At a family reunion in 1983, Baxter Decker, the
author's maternal uncle, who was born in 1909,
agrees to speak — into a cassette recorder — his
recollections of a story told to him by his great-
grandfather, George Barnabas Decker. It is a tale
of a chance encounter in the summer of 1863
during the War between the States.

One / What Baxter was told.

When you come up to the river at floodtide
on a bright summer's day with wind churning
the trees and the marsh water riffling silver
among the cat-tails and no other way across

except the bridge — where it was darkness
on first entering, until your eyes adjusted,
with the gleaming square at the other end,
your horse skittish on the echoing boards —

the thin light coming through cracks, from
all directions, even beneath where you stand
and you can peer down through warped planks
and see water moving — that dizzy sideways

streaming — and at the same time feel wind
slipping through the length of the shaft
strong enough to blow the hat off your head —
then the sense comes to you (even the horse

16

understands, trembling) that the bridge
itself is moving, in long, slow rhythms
like some sort of creaking weathervane
or needle balanced over fields of force —

so when three mounted rebel soldiers stop
at the east-bank entrance, they look inside
and see my great-grandfather with the last
of twenty armloads of brush he has piled

against the center arch so that the draft
will fan the embers straight up to the roof
and fire the cedar shakes. The whole bridge
will last about as long as a pine torch

on election day. He glances up from his work
and sees the rebs reined in, watching. Three
against one, but he knows their saddlebags
are weighted down with slabs of jowl bacon

and coffee-grinders and bolts of calico
and God knows what other kinds of plunder
taken these last ten days. If it comes to a race
he can probably outrun them, even on Old Fly —

who is tethered at the west end, switching
his tail, occasionally nudging gravel loose
from the roadbed — part of the steady stream
of sand and grit and pebbles sifting down

into the waters far below. Starting out
that morning my great-grandfather had stuck
a ball pistol in his belt — the same one
he carried when he rode off to Mexico

with Lew Wallace and the 1st Indiana.
Never fired a shot in that campaign, never
even made it to Buena Vista. Now, it was
too much trouble to load the damned thing.

The rebs are still watching. Rather than
venture onto the bridge, they turn away
from the entrance. "Be a shame to burn such
a fine-lookin' bridge," one of them calls.

Fly shifts around nervously and knocks loose
more pebbles. Except for a tendency to bite
now and then, he was a good horse, not the least
handicapped by being ten years old and owned

by a carpenter and schoolteacher — callings
my great-grandfather followed, when he wasn't
out burning bridges, or trying to save the Union
and the State of Indiana from sure perdition

now that Morgan's raiders had been loosed on
northern soil. My great-grandfather, Barnabas,
has eight sulfur matches in his coat pocket.
He has already spied the bolt on one of the beams

where he intends to strike them, one after
the other, in a wind that continues to howl
the length of the bridge — hoping that he can
cup his fingers around at least one match

and get the conflagration started. Now
the captain (as it turns out) has dismounted
and is walking this way, the new vibrations
spooking Old Fly until my great-grandfather

calls to him, tells him to stop that whining.
He draws the pistol and lays it on a side brace.
The captain comes on, slowly, up to where
all the brush is stacked. He wears a uniform

so smudged you can't tell what army he's in.
His eyes are bloodshot; he hasn't shaved or
slept in five days. Two bars and a plated sword.
Touches his hat. "Sir, would you happen to be

a gambling man?" George Barnabas Decker nods.
The captain smiles. "That's good to know.
My men back there had a mind to ride in here
and shoot you. Fortunately, I dissuaded them.

It has always been my concern that politics
not come before good manners. We have been
out for a look at your state, and I must say
it is exceptionally handsome. But to business:

You have my personal word that General Morgan
has no intention of riding in this direction.
I am equally confident that you are under orders
to let nothing stop you from burning this bridge.

Therefore" — and as though plucked from the air,
a deck of cards appeared in his right hand —
"I propose we cut for high card. You win,
I and my troopers withdraw, so that you may

continue to carry out your orders. I win,
and you cease and desist." At this, Old Fly
lingeringly broke wind. The captain grinned.
"I was about to say we'd take your horse, too,

but now that he has come out so strongly
for Union, I am not sure he could be trusted.
You may keep your horse, sir. But if you lose,
you will withdraw, giving us your word of honor

that the bridge will not be harmed, insofar
as it is in your power to protect it. You may
tell your commander that you were driven off
by a superior force, against considerable odds."

Two / What Barnabas said.

"Now, I helped build that bridge, as a young man,"
Barnabas told me, many years later, "working
for Old Man Hogsett, who spit tobacco juice
on the bolts, for grease, while we tightened

them up. Spent two long, blistering months
on a crew of six, fitting those big timbers,
wading up to my ass in all that mud, getting
kicked and bit by those damned bluenose mules

and all the time that old man cussing me out,
slobbering brown spit everywhere, and swearing
I'd never be a carpenter's apprentice in hell.
I tell you I was damned unhappy to see that reb

bring out that deck of cards. That morning,
when the mayor told me to get down there,
I was looking forward to burning that bridge.
To make matters worse, as a young roustabout

I had played faro and low ball and blackjack
up and down both sides of the Ohio River
as far south as Cairo, and I knew a tin-plated
smooth-talking Kentucky card-shark the minute

he opened his mouth. Had a better chance
of cutting that bridge loose and floating it
downriver and giving it to Jeff Davis himself
than I did drawing high card against that

back-room bushwhacker from Bowling Green.
'Surely you'll allow me to cut the cards?'
I said in my best riverboat gambler's voice.
The captain leaned over and laid the deck

on one of those twelve-inch hand-dressed beams,
alongside that damned empty pistol. Right away
the wind whipped the first two or three cards
off the deck and blew them on down the bridge

but the captain never turned a hair. I saw
that tucked in his sash he had a horse pistol
with a bore as big as one of those bridge bolts;
it occurred to me he did not go about with

this piece unloaded. More cards kept blowing
away and he just stood there, waiting for me
to move. I reached out and stopped the cards
from blowing, then cut them with one hand.

He nodded and smiled, and I took off the six
of diamonds. He started to take a card, but
at that moment the other two rebs rode up,
their stolen appaloosas moving like smoke.

They'd been out reconnoitering the east bank;
now they dismounted at the entrance. Suddenly
a gust of wind lifted the deck into the air.
'I'll get them cards for you, Sir!' the boy

called out, but the captain raised a hand.
'That was our last deck,' he said, watching
the cards flutter away. He turned to me:
'How many matches have you got?' 'Only eight,'

I said. 'That's all I could find this morning.'
'Well then,' he said, 'it's settled. It's
the bridge against Fate, in a howling gale.
Each of us has two tries to light the pile.'

They commenced to bet among themselves,
rummaging through their pockets, finding
jack-knives and cameo rings and ivory combs.
The boy even had a horned toad in a cigar box

but they made him throw it away, nudge it
through a broken place in the bridge floor.
'It will be perfectly all right down there,'
the captain assured him. Finally they were ready.

The captain and the boy bet against the bridge,
the older man for it. The captain asked me
for the matches. He gave back two, passed
four out to the men, kept the last two himself.

The boy gave a rebel yell and got down
and scrunched up a handful of dead leaves
and after a bad start managed to get it going
with the second match, even making some smoke

before the wind blew it out. The older man,
who looked like he wanted do it the easy way
and shoot me on the spot — he simply struck
both matches and tossed them toward the pile.

The captain frowned. Now it was my turn.
I opened my coat against the wind and snapped
the match with my thumbnail, and got it
going good, then knelt, still holding it,

and reached it over to the pile; in the next
instant the wind snuffed it out. One down.
Stepping forward, the captain produced a bill
from his waistcoat, and held it up: bank note

recently stolen and already worthless, from
the looks of it. He wadded it up, struck a match
and got it going, then tossed it onto the brush
where it began to uncurl, burning all the while.

Old Fly, made nervous by the strange horses
tied at the east end of the bridge, chose
this particular moment to rear and whinny,
and the rebel mounts began to stamp and neigh.

One of the ponies skittered onto the bridge;
twigs from the pile fell through the cracks,
scattering onto the river below. The captain
and I each had one match left. The wind

was at gale force now, we could hear it
whipping through the trees on both sides
of the river, and rattling the loose shingles.
He knelt, in his spurred boots and greatcoat,

using his hat to shield the flame that sprang
from his last match. 'Hit's a-goin' t' go!'
the boy called, and we all leaned down but
the leaves were too green, the wind too strong;

wisps of smoke curled and blew away. 'Well sir,'
the captain said, turning to me. 'Your turn.
You have the last match, I believe.' I did,
and when I held it up thunder and lightning

broke simultaneously in the sky above our heads
as though I had drawn them down — the storm
the mayor had warned me about finally arrived,
sheets of rain suddenly lashing at the roof

and walls of the bridge, the horses like to
jumping out of their skins the way everything
began swaying back and forth. 'We better be
gettin' off this here bridge!' the older man

shouted, but the captain, as if hypnotized
by that last match, stood firm: the light
in his eyes was that of a man who has stayed —
seen and raised every bet on the table,

and then called, earned the right to see
what you've got in the hole. 'Mighty handsome
bridge,' he said, scratching his nose but still
keeping his eye on me and that matchstick.

'Nothing comparable down where we come from.'
'That's for damn sure,' the older man said.
The boy said nothing. They all looked at me.
Fly looked like he was about ready to sneeze.

Summer storms are peculiar — the way a wind
as strong as a cyclone can blow one minute
and then get still the next. The rain stopped
all of a sudden, and we could hear the horses

whickering, sand sifting through the cracks,
the sound of water whirling below us. I struck
the match. It burned steady as a wax candle
on Easter morning. It even made light there

in all those shadows. The captain took off
his hat. The two scouts stood beside him.
'Go ahead,' he said. I turned with the match
and put it to the nest of leaves, where flames

fairly leapt up into the brush, crackling and
snapping. The boy and the older man whooped
and hollered and took off for their horses.
This spooked Fly, who reared and broke loose

and came thundering through the bridge past
the place where we stood, as though he were
hell bent on having a bite of rebel horseflesh.
The captain and I ran, too, clear to the east fork,

where we could look back and see the fire
rising and spreading and going good now.
The boy caught up with Fly and gentled him
and brought him over to me. We mounted up.

Once I was in the saddle I was confounded
when the captain reached out and handed me
the ball pistol I had plumb forgot and left
back there to burn up in the flames. I told you

he was a sly one; I knew that, the minute
I laid eyes on him. After the older man
had paid up what he lost, the scouts galloped
ahead, on out of sight. We rode for a piece

in the drizzle of rain. It was letting up.
We could look back and see clouds of smoke
boiling from the center of the bridge. Flames
broke out here and there among the shakes.

'Well,' the captain said, 'I'm much obliged.
I'll trade this old buck knife back to him
before we reach the Ohio line. But I'm still ahead
by half a slab of bacon, and this turnip watch.

And you, sir, far from having diverted
General Morgan and his notorious raiders,
have set fire to a bridge that half the county
depended on to get their goods to market.'

I nodded but said nothing. 'I must say,'
he went on, 'you're a likeable fellow.
And a gambler to boot. I'm truly sorry
I can't take you prisoner. No point in that,

however, since we'll all be prisoners
before this is over. That, or corpses,
moldering in our graves.' He smiled
to himself, as though recognizing where

that last phrase had come from. 'So far,
we haven't had much luck at persuading
any of you Hoosiers to go along with us.'
'No,' I told him, 'but it would look better

if I had to walk back home.' 'Precisely,'
he said. 'As though you had struggled
against a superior force, and succeeded,
firing the bridge despite considerable odds.'

He glanced at Fly. 'That's not much of a horse.
Don't look like conscript material to me.
What's his name?' 'Fly. Old Fly.' 'Had him
long?' 'Seven years,' I said. 'He minds.'

'We'll take him along for a few miles,' he said.
'Won't be the war's first escaped prisoner.
He'll probably be home along about sundown.'
Behind us, the bridge crossbeams were yellow

with fire. The sky was beginning to clear.
We reached a bend in the road, and stopped.
The captain sat on his horse, looking back
at the burning bridge. 'War,' he said.

'A tragic and senseless affair. I've found
there's no way to get through such stupidity
unless a man can make a wager now and then
on something that don't matter anyhow,

one way or the other. I'll tell you what.
I'll bet you a quarter-eagle gold piece
that Old Fly here beats you home.' We both
laughed. At that instant Fly stretched over

and tried to bite his horse. I drew him in,
and got him settled down, then slipped
out of the saddle and handed the reins up
to the captain. To my surprise he leaned down

suddenly, the way a born cavalryman can do,
and embraced me, as though we were old friends
saying goodbye, parting for the last time.
He straightened up, touched the brim of his hat,

and rode off briskly, drawing Fly behind him.
When I got back to town the mayor came out
to meet me, wearing his Mexican War uniform.
Fly had turned up half an hour earlier,

and they were starting to get worried. I had
fired the bridge, like they said, and wanted
only to go home. Next day they claimed I was
a hero, and deserved a medal, but I laughed

and told them they'd sing a different tune
when it came time to sell the hogs. Besides,
details from Gettysburg were coming in,
and they had other things to think about."

Three / Going fishing.

It wasn't until seven years later, when Grant
was in the White House, that Schuyler Colfax —
whose sister lived in Mississinewa County —
shook loose the money to build a new bridge.

It was a trestle bridge made of iron girders,
a quarter mile upstream from the point
where the old bridge stood. Barnabas Decker,
who watched it being built, and made sure

they did it right, lived on until 1920,
and died in his ninetieth year. Summer days
during the First War he used to take me fishing
off that iron bridge, and he would point out

the two limestone piers — the middle one gone —
where the covered bridge once stood. He would
help me bait my hook, and show me how to cast
my line out toward the most promising pools.

We would lean on the struts, keeping an eye
on our bobbers, and he would tell the story
of how he fired the first bridge, and saved
the town of Somerset from sure destruction

at the hands of the rebel invasionary force.
And if I didn't catch anything, sometimes
he would take out the thick leather wallet
he carried, and sort through all the bills

and clippings and membership cards in lodges
that hadn't held a meeting in twenty years,
and find, somewhere in that mass of papers,
wrapped squarely in what he called "a piece

of foolscap" — would actually let me hold
in my hand a creased, worn playing card,
so dim and faded it might have been a six
of diamonds, once upon a time, but now

looked more like an ace. "I forgot to ask,"
he explained once, "whether it was ace high,
and when I cut the deck the first time,
I palmed the top card. Any time you get

a chance to take out a little insurance,
never hesitate. I mean, the man was clearly
a Kentuckian, you could tell by the way
he sat his horse, the first time they rode up."

He laughed and readjusted his cane pole.
"Been just my luck, if I'd asked him,
he would have said it was ace low.
That's how we used to play down at Cairo.

So I showed him the six. Either way,
he probably had half the deck up his sleeve.
You know how those Kentuckians are. You
can't trust 'em, even when they're standing

right in front of you." I was just a boy,
eight or nine years old, leaning against
a rusty girder, listening to old Barnabas
half talking to himself, half entertaining me

with his war stories. But I can still recall
looking downriver, on those bright afternoons,
when a sudden wind might come up, rippling
the trees and turning everything to silver,

and I remember thinking that at such moments
I could almost see those cards blowing away —
watch them scattering down the tunnel and on
through the cracks in those boards: see them

tumbling and falling through the air toward
the water, showing one last hand — queens
and eights and a one-eyed jack — and then
landing on the water and disappearing there —

all except this one card my great-grandfather
had kept with him, all these years, that I
could hold in my hand, and touch, and feel
the softness of, while he told the story again.

It was that card that was buried with him,
finally, in an inner pocket of his black suit,
along with his ball pistol, and a turnip watch
on a gold chain that turned out to be brass —

a watch he always said never did work anyhow
but which he had borrowed, from a friend,
years before, without really intending to,
in case Old Fly never found his way back home.

Visit

Whatever day you choose, rain will be falling
out of that granite sky. Whatever path
you take will make no sound. A lone bird calling
through the double row of hemlocks seems half
silenced by the gathering mist. Within,
the house is still, and someone takes your coat
and shows you through the rooms. Here she had been
a child, then a woman, one who scribbled notes
on scraps of butcher paper. Here is her room —
the paisley shawl across the bed, the desk —
and here, in a closet opened for you now,
one of her muslin dresses. In the rain's gloom
you study the shape of the sleeves, the neck,
the bodice and the slim waist. You know how

but not why. For that, go back to the hall
where earlier you saw an old map of the town
a bird's-eye view, in steep perspective, all
shown at a glance — and shrink yourself down
not to that scale but to that time, that place:
pasture and meadow surround the house, trees
shade every path, all things move at the pace
of the sun. Suddenly, skirt hiked to her knees,
shoes kicked aside, she begins to run through
the hayfield, through deep grass, laughing,
calling to others behind her — a loon's cry,
a fierce joy! Gradually coming into view,
her father and older brother go by, passing
without a word. You begin to understand why.

Follow her now, as she leaves the house, climbs
into a carriage, ready to spend a year
at Mount Holyoke Seminary. The times
are troubling: a Baptist preacher spies fear
in the Book of Daniel, the faithful advance
to rooftops for the World's End, Shaker girls
babble in strange tongues while elders prance
on mountainsides. Amid the smoke and swirl
of anti-slavery politics and talk of war
in Mexico, she takes tea with the headmistress,
who explains: Sunday nights in the main hall
the student body assembles; on the floor
a minister chalks a line. Each will profess
her sins and her depravity, then all

will sing hosannas as each passes over
to be saved. The year progresses in this way;
two hundred girls burning with the fever
of salvation cross the line. Then comes a day
in March, when the strange one, Emily
Dickinson, stands alone at the last meeting,
facing them all. Miss Lyon's "family"
huddles in the bleak hall, rain sleeting
the windows, and one iron stove, banked low.
Swaying back and forth in the shifting gloom
above her head, four brassbound lamps cast
quavering light. Something begins to grow
in that unsteadiness — a constancy, a doom
stronger than all their pieties. And lasts.

A poet's life is simply told: the task
of waiting, and of writing down; and listening,
while the visitors come and go. They bask
in talk, and laughter; she sees a glimmering
in the hallway mirror. Rather than a master,
she comes to know herself. In the long days
of silence, and solitude, nothing faster

33

than her pen inches across the page — stays
for a moment — moves on. A clock chimes.
She rises, goes down to the kitchen to check
the bread baked earlier that morning. Feels
it's cooled enough. Rain by evening. Lines
the basket with a clean white cloth, stacks
the brown loaves inside. Their fragrance heals.

The house and grounds become her world: the path
out through the apple trees, the summer porch,
the upstairs room from which to watch the last
friend, waving goodbye; or the faint torch
flickering out, to mark the holiday's end
on the village common. Not growing old,
she simply dematerializes, sends
the best part away, hides it under folds
of linen in the basket, or in the desk.
When there was music in the drawing room,
she listened from the top of the stairs;
When the house was quiet again, the risk
remained — to have no presence, to assume
all, everything, to be lighter than air.

But can we know such things, or is it true
the face you thought you saw in the glass assumed
a shape you wanted to see — your own? And who
or what she was, and whether she still presumes
on days like this to drift on down the stairs,
staying a room or two ahead, lifting the hem
of her dress, making no sound, as though air
were what she fed on — all that grows dim
in the evening shadows. Whatever remains,
whatever you hoped to find by coming here
(the path through the meadow, the lone bird's
cry, the shawl on the bed) is dark with rain.
Now you must go. What's lost will reappear —
will come back even stronger. In her words.

Catalpa

Of the trumpet-creeper family, with cordate leaves
and pale, showy flowers in terminal racemes. From
the Creek word *kutuhlpa*, literally, "head with wings."

He was just a farm hand, almost a drifter,
but one who had been in the neighborhood
for a long time, working on different farms.
He was always part of the threshing crew,
no matter where you went. In the winter
he would be there in the general store,
sitting back by the stove. He was afflicted,
in a strange way, and people left him alone,
for the most part. They looked after him, too.

It always seemed to happen right around
the time of the year when you see the first
lightning bugs — we would be out cutting hay,
getting ready to bring it in — somewhere along
about the middle of June. It didn't matter
how much water he drank, or didn't drink,
what he had for breakfast, what kind of hat
he wore: a time always came when he felt
the sunstroke coming back.
                              He told us once
he could look out across the field and see
what seemed to be a squall line moving in,
heading his way — except that it was empty,
there was nothing behind it.
                              He would turn
so we couldn't see his face, and begin
to moan — the way a preacher, breaking off

the service, will start speaking in the tongues —
and in the next instant he would light out
for the woods near the creek.

                         We let him go
because we had seen it before, we knew
it was happening again. It was time
for him to go out there and look around
for something we couldn't see — he called it
finding the monkey.

                         He swore up and down
it was the only thing that could save him.
It was something his grandfather told him,
when he was small, that he read in a book
or maybe *Harper's Weekly* — that said back
before the first white man came, if you stood
right at the point where the Allegheny
meets the Monongahela — where Pittsburgh
got started, later on — where the Ohio River
begins — then all that country west of there
contained the biggest stand of hardwood trees
the world had ever seen. And if you took
a monkey, and put it up in the nearest tree,
that monkey would be able to make it
all the way to the Mississippi River
without touching ground.

                         Most times he stayed
till dusk in the deepest part of the woods
where the catalpas were blooming — out there
with those enormous white flowers rising
high above him like waves starting to crest —
and all their blossoms would be sending down
perfume, and drawing clouds of bumblebees,
and moths, and hummingbirds, all of them
feeling their way into those flowers, and if
you were up high enough and could have seen

inside them, the throats of those flowers
would be all streaked and dotted with purple
and brown and yellow, and full of light.

According to what he had told us already —
back before the War, on the old home place,
when he was barely old enough to read,
that same grandfather took him by the hand
and led him out across the last big stretch
where they were clearing off the bottomland
along the Massasauga River, right close
to where it joined with the Mississinewa —
where mule teams had dragged the last big trees
into windrows, and where the fire had burned
for days, sending up sheets of smoke and flame.
They walked among great smoldering stumps
while the old man said the names of the trees
and the boy came after him, listening to him
call them out, in a voice like judgment day —
the different maples, the oaks, the hornbeam,
the beech, the yellow poplar, even the walnut —
and the old man wept as he said their names,
and sat down on a log, and the boy could not
console him, and did not know what was wrong.

Finally, toward evening, at milking time,
somebody would be sent out to find him,
and he would be propped on a log under
a big catalpa, with a few lightning bugs
starting to show, and the air turned cool,
the sun almost down, unable to reach him now.
He would be all right, ready to come home,
not saying much on the way back. We knew
he would be fine for the rest of the year.

If you were the one who had been sent out
to find him —
                    when you got there, when you came
along the path, you could look up and see
catalpa blossoms heavy with pollen
and starting to close — even a few petals
worked loose, drifting down around the place
where he sat waiting — and you might suppose
that something had passed over him, up high,
where the big flowers were thickest —
                                        some gust
of wind that had already blown through, some
tremor in the leaves —
                        and whatever it was,
however long it lasted, he had been there
when it happened, he had seen it or at least
sensed its presence. Some part of him knew
it would happen — the way he remembered it
back when the big trees were still standing.
He was drawn there each time without knowing
why or what it was, what it had been once,
what it might become again.
                            And whether
all of this was caused by the first sunstroke
years ago, that still would creep back over him
each summer, that always seemed to find him —
none of us knew, least of all did he know
himself.
        But he sensed what he had become.
Part of him was in tune with hidden things,
and this was the way they worked together
when the sun stood directly overhead
and trees creaked in the wind, and blossoms
shook with an unseen rain, and something
seemed to be moving among the leaves —
trumpet-creeper, catalpa, *head with wings*.

Recollections
of a contingent of Coxey's Army
passing through Straughn, Indiana,
in April of 1894

> More than 2,500,000 men walked the streets in search of work
> in the terrible winter of 1893-94. . . . It was only when
> government failed to act that angry men began to take matters
> into their own hands.
>
> In Massillon, Ohio, Jacob S. Coxey set about organizing a
> massive march on Washington. . . . On Easter Sunday . . . 100
> men set out for the Capitol, accompanied by half as many
> reporters. . . . No less than seventeen armies set out for
> Washington in the spring of 1894.
>
> Harold U. Faulkner
> *Politics, Reform and Expansion: 1890-1900*

There by the rail fence in that lost, broken light, that moment
still wavering like a loose ribbon: whether she remembers most
the sound of their singing, or their march through the wagon ruts,
the angry crowd, the elm trees with their great curved branches —

"They cain't be for Coxey, he done got killed a long time ago!"
somebody called out. She remembered it was cold, she could see
her breath, how scared she became when her brothers threw rocks,
how her father cuffed them, while the marshal waved back the crowd —

and on they came, in ragged double file along the National Road,
none of them in step, some reaching to take an apple or a crust
of bread held out for them. It was the first time she recalled
seeing black skin — a man, striding along, paying them no mind —

and in this way they slogged on past the store-fronts and taverns,
past the young doctor reined in and saluting — near the station
a preacher waving his hat, then running to heave a brick at them —
finally only children still following, pretending they had joined —

until they drew abreast of the Tipton place, with its stone wall,
the last house in town, only bare fields ahead of them now —
and she saw a stack of hedgeapples, sheltered by the stones,
that had lasted the winter, and hurried over to gather some —

made an apron with her skirt, as her grandmother had taught her,
and ran along the main road, calling after them until someone
looked around — a gray-haired man in a faded blue coat with badges
on the lapels, tarnished buttons, one arm pinned at the shoulder —

who with his left hand took the sodden green fruit she held out,
stuffing his pockets, nodding gravely, saying nothing she could
remember in later years, but finally reaching down to press
her fingers, then hurrying on, turning back once to wave to her.

Mussel Shell
with Three Blanks Sawed Out

There were these two men heard Dude Holcomb
found a big freshwater pearl and counted on
taking it over to Terre Haute, and selling it
to a gypsy woman he knew there.
                              This pearl
was half an inch thick, and shaped like a teardrop.
Dude liked to say it was the color of the inside
of a water moccasin's mouth.   It earned him
a certain amount of attention. People came up
and asked him about it, at the general store.
He carried it in his watch pocket, wrapped up
in a piece of felt. But he'd get it out sometimes.
I didn't know exactly what Dude would do
if somebody tried to make off with that pearl,
but I hoped he had some sort of plan.
                              Me and Dude
was business partners. After I joined up with him,
I spent the better part of three whole summers
wading the Mississinewa River, dredging up
mussels. Dude taught me everything there is
to know about shell fishing. It's not something
people knew much about, even in those days.
Dude always said that if you could find shell,
you could get by. That was his philosophy:
getting by.
                In Somerset, back in those days,
just before the First War, except for the farmers
and the people who lived in town and worked
at the mill, there wasn't much to do. Nobody
out along the river had a trade to speak of. None

of Dude's friends had regular jobs. You'd work
for a day or two, whatever might come along,
maybe putting up a stretch of fence, or helping
roof a barn, and then you'd loaf for a few days.
If you got short of money, you'd ask around,
go talk to a few people you knew, and finally
rustle up something else to do.
                              Dude Holcomb
did a bit of farming, but most of the time, year
in and year out, he was off somewhere, fishing.
He fished in rivers and lakes and ponds, or out
on the ice, with most anything that came to hand,
whether it was worms, crickets, or dough balls.
Whatever was out there, he'd catch — turtle,
bluegill, striped bass, muskie, channel cat.
He always had a couple of trot-lines going.
In the spring he knew the best places to find
morels, and he had a sharp eye for ginseng.
He wore cast-off clothes, and he usually kept
a chaw of Mail Pouch tobacco in his right cheek.

People on the river said when he went after
frog legs, he didn't bother with a jacklight.
He liked to go out when the moon was full.
When he found the proper target, he'd rare back
and let fly a stream of pure tobacco juice
that could hit a bullfrog right between the eyes
from ten feet away. Folks said it was either
the nicotine, or the shock of it all, would stop
that bullfrog dead in its tracks. Then Dude
would wade over and scoop it up in his net.
I heard he could do that, but I never saw it.
I believed it, though.
                              Dude was somewhere around
sixty years old. He lived by himself, in a cabin,
on forty acres of bottomland he had inherited

from his father. I remember that place well.
It was on the other side of Lost Bridge, down
the South River Road. I was fourteen or fifteen.
This was along about nineteen-sixteen. They said
there was a war on somewhere, but it seemed
like it hadn't found its way to wherever we were.
My mother had died, and my father had run off.
There were three of us kids. We got parceled out.
My sisters got sent to Fort Wayne. My Aunt Mae
took me in. I was old enough to do the chores —
chop wood, split kindling, carry out the ashes.

My aunt was married to a man named Kercheval,
who owned a half share in a dry-goods store.
He suggested that I call him Uncle Harve.
Him and Dude had gone to school together
in a one-room schoolhouse, somewhere up
in Prophet Township, on the Massasauga.
He had always thought highly of Dude Holcomb.
He assured me that Dude was a smart man.
In fact, he believed there were many things
a boy my age could learn from a man like that.
My aunt had a different opinion. She didn't like it,
but my uncle didn't care — those summer mornings
I got up before daylight, and packed a lunch,
and walked all the way out to Dude's cabin,
along the back roads that followed the river,
to find out what we were going to do that day.

Like I said, for three summers, if the weather
was good, we'd go out and dredge up mussels.
I supplied most of the labor, and Dude provided
the technical supervision. Dude already had
this flat-bottom skiff, but it didn't weigh much,
and we had his old wagon to haul it around in.
Early of a morning the two of us would show up

at a likely spot somewhere on the riverbank.
We'd launch the skiff, and I would get behind it
and push it through the shallows.
                                    Mussels favor
a flat, sandy bottom, and not too much current.
They're social. They grow in patches, and there's
all kinds of mussels — heelsplitters and muckets,
and washboards and pigtoes. I'd just be feeling
around down there, with my bare feet, and when
I ran across a nest of them, I'd bring them up
with the pitchfork, and throw them in the skiff.
Meanwhile, Dude would go on downstream
with the wagon, maybe a quarter mile or so,
and he would unload his tin box, and drag it
down to the edge of the river. Now, this box
was about three feet wide and five feet long,
maybe eight inches high. I don't know whether
he made it himself or somebody made it for him.
He would scoop out a place in the riverbank,
and set that box in there, and leave a space
underneath to put some wood in, and get a fire
going good.
                    Dump in those mussels, and after
they'd been in that boiling water for a while,
they'd open up. We'd dip out the hot water
and pour in the cold. When they cooled enough
to handle, we'd start running them. That meant
we broke them, one at a time, ran our fingers
around inside the shell, took the meat out, felt
for the pearl. Once in a while there might be
a decent pearl in there. But most of the time
if you found anything at all, it was a slug —
a slug was pearl with an odd shape, or a flaw,
but there was still a decent market for slugs.
Dude knew where to go, and how to sell them.
A river pearl looks just like any other pearl,

whether you got it in Japan or anywhere else.
Every year he'd find two or three pearls the size
of a marble shooter. That's what kept him going.
We threw all the meat in a bucket, and sold it
to a farmer Dude knew, who fed it to his hogs.
But there was another way to make money
from mussels, and that's what we did next.

You know the road into Wabash from the south,
down the big hill, right at the bottom? Well,
if you turn right, there's this grassy place —
that was where the old button factory stood.
People took mussel shell there all summer long,
by the wagonload, and after the scale man
weighed you out, he would give you a ticket
you took up front to the head cashier, inside
a wire cage — and they paid thirty dollars a ton,
which was awful good money in those days.
Eventually the shells got made into buttons.
The workers had machines that could reach
down into those shells and saw the blanks out.
It wasn't a punch, and it wasn't a drill, either;
it was some kind of saw. It was powered
with a treadle, just like a sewing machine.

Dude paid me half of whatever a load of shell
would fetch, and during those three summers
I saved up a hundred and eighty-five dollars.
Aunt Mae had me put it in a bank account.
It was my ambition, when I got older, to own
a button factory. That's what I was saving for.
My Uncle Harve thought it was a good idea.
I liked to think I'd be a rich man someday,
but to tell the truth, most of the time, when
I was gathering mussels on the Mississinewa
with Dude Holcomb, it was so much fun
it really didn't seem like work.

Back in those days
there would be whole families come to camp
along the riverbank. That was how they took
their vacations. They'd stay for a week or two,
they'd pitch some kind of army tent or lean-to,
and there would be little kids, and older kids,
boys my own age. The father, he'd get up early
and go off to some cove, and bring back a string
of catfish, for the women to fix for breakfast,
and while they were cleaning the fish, the rest
of the family would be out there on the river,
hunting for mussels. They wanted to find shell,
just like we did, and make some money, and pay
for their vacation that way.

Me and Dude, we'd
stop and talk to them, show them the best beds,
maybe loan them the fork, even let them use
the skiff. We'd tell them how to recognize
different mussels — how to know ebony shell
from monkeyface, and why you never forked
pimplebacks, and why yellow sandshell made
the best pearls. We explained why the factory
wouldn't take purple wartybacks, but wartybacks
still made good pearls.

There was a lot to know,
and I met a lot of pretty girls that way, talking
to them about mussels, and the river, and places
where they ought to look. Sometimes they'd offer
to help. Other times, they'd watch from the shore.
There's just nothing like it, early some morning
in July or August, being out there on the river,
where it's cool and shadowy, and you're moving
knee-deep in the shallows, nudging the skiff
a bit ahead of you, and there's a layer of mist
out over the water, where the sun's rays start
to reach down through, and you can hear voices

46

everywhere around you — young people laughing
and splashing and talking, and up on the bank
somebody's got a fire going, and you can smell
biscuits, and fresh coffee, and catfish frying,
and you've got the whole day ahead of you,
just being out on that river.
                                My Uncle Harve
liked to hear that I was learning useful things
being partners with Dude, out on the river.
But he used to warn me, too: there's always
a few people who don't want to work at all.
Instead, what they want is to come along
and take whatever you got. Like those two men
I started to tell you about, who heard the rumor
that some old man had found a big pearl.
                                            One day
the two of them came crashing down the bank
just when we were running a batch of mussels.
We had been working that stretch for a week,
and we had close to a wagon-load of shell,
up on the road, ready to cash in. But it wasn't
mussel shell those two characters were after.
They grabbed Dude and started shaking him,
and I lit out and climbed up a catalpa tree.
But I could hear them cursing and shouting
while they knocked him around: "Old man,
you better tell us where it is!" A pearl that fine
was worth two, three hundred dollars. I hated
to think of Dude giving it up. They had him
down on the ground, tearing at his clothes,
turning out his pockets, trying to find where
he had put that big pearl. I was about ready
to call down to them and tell them we had it
buried back at the cabin, I'd show them where,
if they'd turn him loose. But they stood him
back on his feet and were trying to shove him
face down in the box full of boiling water.

47

I thought for sure they would kill him. But
in the next instant, a bunch of fishermen
who were camping out in tents, just around
the next bend — they had heard the commotion,
and they came running up the beach — people
who knew Dude, and cared about him — women
with frying pans, men with skinning knives —
screaming for the two men to stop. When I saw
they had turned Dude loose, I shinnied down
from the tree. Dude was already on the ground.
They smashed the tin box and kicked in the skiff,
and then they ran up the bank and disappeared.

It took a while, but all of us together managed
to bring Dude around, and got him to sit up.
He was clearly in a bad way. I never saw a man
open his eyes and look so disillusioned. The skiff
was kindling, and the tin box was all stove in.
But the wagon was all right, and Dude's horse,
Buster, had been up on the road all that time,
and never got a scratch. The summer people said
they'd take Dude back to their camp, but I knew
he'd be better off in his cabin. They helped me
carry him up to the wagon, and get him situated
in the bed, so he could ride easy. I thanked them,
and got up and took the reins.
                              Dude didn't say much
on the way home. It took me about an hour
to get there. He had a room just off the kitchen,
where he slept on this big walnut four-poster
that had been in his family for a hundred years.
Scattered around the room were all manner
of strange things he had collected — wasps' nests
and tortoise shells, and a ladderback chair,
rescued from a steamboat disaster, back
in his father's time.

I got him out of his overalls
and eased him onto the bed. It was right then
I noticed he still had that quid of Mail Pouch
stuck in his cheek. "Do a feller a good turn,"
he said, "and fetch me that there coffee can."
He pointed under the bed, where he kept
a rusty old can.   He took out that big chaw
and dropped it in the juice. Next, he wanted me
to go up to the loft, to get a mess of cobwebs,
to make a poultice for his face.

                        Right outside,
I heard someone holler. It was Harve Kercheval.
A neighbor had come running to the store
with news about the robbery, when the two men
had finally been put to flight. Uncle Harve
had slipped out of his apron and sent a boy over
to the livery stable, to rent him a rig. He drove
all that way, just to make sure I was all right.
Already I had a good idea that my Aunt Mae
would take a dim view of the day's events.
She had been telling my uncle all summer long
that it was about time for me to earn my keep
by clerking in the family store.

                        Nevertheless,
before we finally left for home, I managed
to persuade Uncle Harve to stay for a spell,
and keep watch on Dude, while I took Buster
and drove that last load of shell up to Wabash,
and sold it. I knew it would take a few days
for Dude to get back on his feet. I figured
he could use the money.

                        I didn't suspect it
at the time, but that was the last occasion
I would have anything to do with mussel shells.
Well, maybe I did know, after all. Next door
to the factory was a mound about as tall as a house,

where they threw the used shells after the blanks
had been sawed out. While I was waiting there
for the scale man to write out the weigh ticket,
I picked up a shell — they call it a holey shell —
and put it in my pocket.

      I've kept it all this time.
Here, you can see how the operator sawed out
three blanks, each the size of a silver dime,
from this one shell. What kind of shell is it?
Well, it's a washboard.

      I've kept it all these years,
and I still get it out sometimes, just to feel
the inside, all smooth and shiny, and the outside,
with the lines and blisters, and the growth rings,
and the three holes sawed through. It helps me
remember, even now, about all the good times
we used to have on the river, when I was young,
helping Dude run his trot-lines, and fishing
for turtles, and learning just about everything
there was to know about mussels.

      Right now,
I'm a lot older than Dude ever lived to be.
I've seen a lot of changes during my lifetime.
And I remember how everything changed,
right after that, especially in my own life —
first, when they made me clerk in that store,
and second, when my real father showed up,
and took me and my sisters to live with him
down in Evansville. I hardly ever got back
to Mississinewa County, except now and then,
when I was just passing through.

      But when I did,
I'd make a point of going out to see Dude again,
just to sit with him, there in the cabin, and listen
to his stories. He lasted for another twenty years,
since he was good at finding ways to get by.

He went right on farming his daddy's old place
and kept it mostly in field corn. A man can get
fifty, sixty bushel of corn an acre, and sell it
in the fall, he'll do all right. A piece of ground
like that will see you through some hard times.
About the only thing you need to buy is oil
for the lamp, and matches, and a little salt.
You can grow everything else, or catch it.
Dude always had a big garden, and he kept on
fishing. Even ran a trap line now and then,
sold a few mink and marten pelts each spring.
He just hung on that way till the day he died.

But there was one thing he wouldn't talk about,
and that was what happened to mussel fishing
after the Depression hit, along about thirty-one
or thirty-two — when they learned how to make
buttons out of plastic, and everything changed
practically overnight.
                    All the ways a man could make
a living gathering mussel shells, all of that went
straight down the drain. All the factories shut down,
and all the folks like Dude stopped forking mussels
out of the river. And nobody knew anything at all
about freshwater pearls, or what to do with them,
even if you found one. When I would stop to visit,
we never talked about what happened. Dude knew.
But it probably hurt too much to think about it.

It's all forgotten now.   To make matters worse,
a few years ago they went and built that reservoir,
and covered it up — the river itself, and the towns
and the bridges, and everything that ever was,
down in that valley. That was after Dude's time,
and in a way, I'm glad he never lived to see it.
But I remember the way that river used to be.

I saw it, right before it changed. I can still recall
what it was like.
                    Now that they've gone and built
that dam downstream, there's nobody ever again
going to walk through those shallows, or look out
and see that mist rising. But that's all right.
I reckon somewhere in this world there's still
a couple of rivers that look like the Mississinewa
I used to know, and maybe there's a few people left
with sense enough to know what to do with them.
Dude knew what to do with that river. And that
was what Harve Kercheval wanted me to understand,
something he was convinced was worth knowing.
That's partly why, the same afternoon that Dude
got all beat up, my uncle told me to take Buster
and go sell that last load of shell.
                        I got back
along about sundown. The livery-stable horse
had been ground-tied, out near the front gate.
When I pulled up, Uncle Harve came outside,
and we unhitched Buster, and gave him a drink
from the trough. Next, we led him into the shed
to brush him down, and give him some feed and hay.
I tried to help, but my uncle told me to go inside
and see how Dude was doing.
                            I lit a coal-oil lamp
and stood next to the bed. Dude was stretched out
in his underwear. I woke him up, and handed him
the twenty dollars they had paid me for the load.
He tried to give ten back. "No, Dude," I said,
"they stole your pearl, and messed up your face,
and you're going to need something to get by."
He reared up and pointed beneath the bed again.
"Fetch me that there spittoon," he said. I nudged
the can with my foot, but I realized he wanted me

to hand it to him. When I did, he fished around
in the juice for a while, and finally brought up
that same gob of Mail Pouch he had deposited
earlier that afternoon.

                    I feared the day's events
had overwhelmed his mind, and he was going
to put it back in his cheek. Instead, he squeezed,
and something popped out and fell in his hand.
Whatever it was, he took it and polished it
for a few seconds on the wool army blanket.
When he held it up, I saw it was the pearl —
the same pearl those two men had tried to take,
the pearl shaped like a teardrop, with the color
of a water moccasin's mouth.

                    He had stuck it
in with his chaw, the moment he heard them
coming down the bank, and never spit it out,
nor swallowed it, all that time, even when
they were knocking him around — even when
they tried to shove his face in the boiling water.
"Purty, ain't it?" Dude said. He winked at me.
"I never did see a pearl catch the light that way."

It was a long drive back to Somerset, along
the South River Road. My uncle held the reins,
but the horse seemed to recognize the way.
The moon was out, and there were lightning bugs
in the trees, and along the river. We crossed
the first covered bridge, where the water sparkled
going over the rapids. I was so worn out it was all
I could do to hold up my head. At the same time,
I was downright amazed by what had happened.
 "Why did he put it in the coffee can?" I asked.
"And why did he leave it there all that time?
That couldn't have been good for that pearl."

53

With his free hand, my uncle was smoking a cigar.
He took a puff occasionally. It was something
my aunt invariably frowned upon. He puffed
for a moment, and he thought about it. "Because,"
he said, letting the smoke out slowly through
the corners of his mouth, "those same two men,
they might have shown up at the cabin again."
He took another puff. "It was smart of Dude
to wait until dark." We drove along for a while.
Up ahead, the lights of Somerset were beginning
to show through the trees. "Or just maybe,"
he said finally, "maybe it was me he didn't trust,
sitting there watching over him. What if the pearl
was in plain view, and he fell asleep?" He laughed.
"After all, I'm not a country boy any longer.
I'm the one who's from town."

                                     And afterward?
I asked once or twice, but I never did find out
what Dude did with that pearl. He wouldn't tell.
Maybe he sold it to that gypsy in Terre Haute.
Or maybe he took it to somebody in Pearl City.
I always hoped he found a way to keep it, since
it was about the best pearl anybody ever saw,
who fished along that river.

                                  Even when Dude
was an old man, well up in years, and couldn't
get around much, and didn't have many visitors,
I like to believe he still held on to it.

                                     That way,
when he wanted to remember, he could get it out
of a night, and look at it, and polish it a little,
and hold it up to the lamp, to see it catch the light.

Reminiscence

*A suite
for
piano & voice*

THE EASY WINNERS, Section D

You been asking if I knowed him. I knowed him.
I talked to him maybe fifteen, twenty times
before he passed. Used to reach out a match,
help him light his cigar. His hands shook
so bad he couldn't play no more. Come in
every day to get them cigars. Always bought
three for a quarter. Had this jackknife
inlaid with mother-of-pearl; it was old,
somebody give it to him years ago, maybe
his daddy. He'd lay out them three cigars,
cut each one in half. They'd last longer
that way. We didn't know much about him
at first, 'cept he was a sick man, shouldn't
have been out on the street. Had this shuffle
when he walked, like he was trying to push
a broomstick with his toes.

ROSE LEAF RAG, Section A

A sick man,
fixing to die. Had a studio somewhere
on West 133rd. They say he gave lessons,
worked on his opera, but when I saw him
he was past all that. His wife rented rooms
out of this basement apartment. Some days
he didn't have no place to go. He'd come
down to my uncle's tavern, 'bout a block
off Fifth Avenue, north side of East 129th
You know the sort of place it was. Today
they call them neighborhood bars. People
stopped in for this and that, but mostly
just to talk. There was a war going on
over in France. Everybody had opinions —
the ones that stayed home — about what
ought to be done. Seems like people always
talk more during a war. You ever notice?

THE CASCADES, Section B

It was a club. The piano was up on a stage;
at night a man played for dancing. Drinks,

women, cards. It ain't changed much, that day
to this. Afternoons he'd come in and sit
at the bar. Wouldn't drink nothing. Word
got around, who he was. Nobody said much.
He'd talk to the bartender sometimes, maybe
read the *Daily News.* His wife would come in
'long about five or six o'clock, take him
by the hand, lead him on home. He'd been
a handsome man in his prime. Not too tall.
Not more than fifty years old, even then.
Been through some hard times. After I met him
he didn't have but five or six more months.

FIG LEAF RAG, Section D

I was seventeen years old. Come all the way
from Birmingham by myself, on the Flyer,
a week before my tenth birthday. My daddy
got hisself killed, working on the railroad,
my mama couldn't keep me. She handed me up
to the conductor with a one-way ticket
and her sister's address wired to my coat.
Gave me a sack of cornbread to eat on the way.
I lived with her folks up north. Quit school.
First job I ever had, working for my uncle.
Emptied the slops and spittoons, helped out.
In those days I was trying to learn piano.

ORIGINAL RAGS, *Section A*

They let me practice during the day, come in
during the evenings, spell the regular man.
Fancier places was starting to get machines
that made the music. You put in a nickel
and they went like crazy for five minutes,
never got tired. Never got drunk or asked
for more money. People had Victrolas, too,
they could make music that way. Never thought
much about it. I wanted to be a professor
in some fancy place down in Atlantic City,
have all the women fight over me. Figured
I had to break in somewhere. I was just a kid.
Never occurred to me how he started it all —
being able to write down what he heard,
what other folks didn't even know was there.

PINEAPPLE RAG, *Section B*

Some days he'd be sitting at the bar
and I'd be up on the stage, fooling around
on my own. Like I said, he was too sick
to play much anymore. He'd call out things,
try to help me get different chords right.
Used to talk to me about how to put in

58

"the walking bass." That's what he called it.
First time I ever heard about it. That was
ten, twelve years 'fore anybody else
started playing that way, out in Chicago,
or down in Washington, D.C. Eubie Blake,
he claims he heard it there in Baltimore
when he was a boy, but I don't believe him.
Anyway, I picked it up from this man,
I been working it in my stuff ever since.

MAGNETIC RAG, Section C

Sometimes he'd be clear, you understand?
Sometimes he'd not be there at all, he'd be
off in some other place. Nothing to say.
I remember there was a clock on the wall,
an old Seth Thomas, been up there forever.
Bartender wound it first thing every morning.
One day he sat there chewing on his cigar —
half the time he never even had it lit —
and he pointed at that clock. "Young man,"
he said, "the way you play ragtime music
is just the same as what it takes to make
that clock go.

STOPTIME RAG, Section A

When it's stopped, nothing's
happening. To make it run, you got to know
the numbers just like you got to know the notes
and all the chords. You need a key to wind it —
not too hard, not too soft. Put your strength
into it, but don't turn it too tight. Next,
you got to start the pendulum. It goes steady
of its own accord, it's what moves the hands.
Last of all, you got to set the hands. Clock
ain't worth nothing at all if it don't give
the right time. So you got to know what time
it is in the first place. Won't do no good
to wind it up or start the motion, lessen
you know that. Won't do you no good at all."
That's what I remember most of what he said.

WALL STREET RAG, Section D

He only played once or twice. It didn't
come over good. His hands wouldn't be still,
even to light them cigars. Wasn't long before

60

she took him to Ward's Island. He died there;
it was in the papers. I didn't go to the funeral.
Never saw his wife again, either. Right then,
I was fixing to join up. My uncle took me
down to Fort Dix, and they made me a fry cook
in the Rainbow Division. I went to Paris,
sat in with the boys in Jim Europe's band.
Kept on making music, one way or another,
the rest of my life. Must have been forty years
'fore somebody asked about him again. You ain't
the first. But there ain't been all that many
coming in here, asking me if I knowed him.

GLADIOLUS RAG, Section D

Like I been saying, I knowed him fairly well
at the end of his life, and the start of mine.
And I had plenty of time to think about
what he meant that day he tried to explain —
that it really wouldn't work unless you had
the right time. I think he wasn't talking
only about music — stride piano, ragtime,
whatever you want to call it. Same way I think
he wasn't talking only about clock time,
what most folks run their life by, the kind
of time that comes over the radio. I think
he wanted to tell me about something else
and this was the only way he could say it —
how you have to know the time you live in,
how it carries you along.

SCOTT JOPLIN'S NEW RAG, Section A

It must have been
something in the music when he first heard it
back before he learned how to write it down —
something that had already come a long way
to reach out to him, something he understood
would keep on going even after him and me
and everybody else who made that kind of music
was gone. That's what he knew. Something
that drew him on, that held him. When you got
that pendulum going steady in the left hand
and the right hand's working off the beat —
when you shoveled in that last scoop of coal
and you're headin' straight on down the track —
then there's still something else, something
he didn't have no words for, but he wanted me
to know about, to be ready — the way a stranger
ask you for the right time, you don't lie to him.

MAPLE LEAF RAG, Section D

— fine —

Spirea

Then she came, the sybil, out through the doors
of The Bell, the single drinking establishment
permitted in that narrow little country town —
she came out neither staggering nor collapsing
but gliding — not carefully, one step at a time,
like a tight-rope walker, but recklessly, wantonly,
as someone oblivious to danger, who knows already
what lies ahead, and has nothing to fear.
                                    Down
the wooden steps of the board walkway, on down
into the dust and refuse of the street, the rinds
and horse droppings, and they watched her go
without really noticing — since they saw this
every evening, now that warm weather had come,
when she ventured out to wander in the town —
and the fact that she was barefooted, that
she wore only a blue shirtwaist, that her hair
hung the length of her back, and was never combed
or pinned up, that she seldom stopped talking
to herself, that all her relatives were dead,
that she had no place to stay, owned nothing,
needed nothing, harmed no one —
                                    these facts
were accepted, known throughout the community,
were discussed by the ladies' aid society,
by the minister and by the township trustee,
and yet none of them could contain her — not
the bartender, who told her when it was time
to leave, not the old rag buyer, who reined in
his horse, when he saw her, and called to her,
asking her to come sit beside him in the wagon,
and he would take her home — for none of them

would she turn back, even when they pleaded
and called out her name.
                       Each time she went forth,
when she walked through the streets, the alleys,
in the twilight, some of them encountered her —
the husbands out watering their lawns, the wives
with their children, the young people pausing,
at the corner, with their bicycles, watching her,
seeing her go by. Many avoided her passing;
many were afraid, unable to return her bright gaze.
A light shone from her eyes. Something glimmered
when she moved. There was about her a presence,
an immanence, that announced a way, a direction
most of them could not imagine, would never know.
She walked on, heedless, muttering to herself,
leaving them far behind.
                       In this way she journeyed
through the summer evenings, and into the night,
while all around her doors were closing, lamps
were dimmed, the world was preparing for sleep.
Always she moved in a straight line, pausing
for no obstacle, respecting no property line —
through backyards, over fences, across gardens,
managing to steer, nightly, by a different star —
by Venus smoldering low above the line of trees,
by Mars or Saturn in stark opposition to the moon —
by whatever brightness seemed most beckoning,
however faint or furious its glow.
                       In this way
she traversed all points of the town, stopping
sometimes to speak to whomever or whatever
she encountered — whether house, tree, horse
or child — but invariably moving on, walking
on through the streets and into the countryside,
walking out among the fields, the gravel roads,
walking until she collapsed against a stone wall,

under a hedge, or in a barn, with rain falling,
walking until she lost her way among dark dreams.

In this manner, on the first evening in May, drawn
by an unknown star, she leaves the tavern, and comes
eventually to the edge of town, to the side yard —
to the croquet court, actually — of a professor
of physics at the college, who nightly sets up
his reflecting telescope: and who on this evening
has trained it on an elusive entity —
                            a nebula
thousands of light years away, a great star cluster
tilted on one side, displaying vast spiral arms —
it is this same man, this professor, who notices,
behind him, something struggling through the hedge,
through the arms of the spirea called "bridal-veil,"
through that pale maze of blossoming, that thicket
of lush, damp, drooping, spiraling white branches —
not far away in the twilight he hears someone
coming toward him, then recognizes this wanderer
from the town —
                            watches her shoulder aside the canes,
bursting at last onto the level lawn, then stopping,
righting herself, reaching to touch and feel the welts
along her arms, her shoulders, the thin red cut,
on her cheek — observes her peer about, slowly,
at the house, the arbor, the herbs in their ladder,
her gaze turning at last to the well-dressed man
with his celluloid collar, his knotted silk tie,
where he stands with one hand on the telescope.

Is he young, and handsome, is this semester
his first in the town, has he only recently
accepted a position at the little college?

Does he turn the heads of the young ladies,
does he sing bass in the Baptist church choir,
is he one of the town's leading bachelors?
Or is he a white-haired gentleman, stooped,
round-shouldered, has he been there for years,
taught generations of young people, outlived
an affectionate wife, sent forth children,
lived to see grandchildren, does he reside alone
at the edge of town, on a wide brick street,
in a gas-boom mansion with a massive hedge
of spirea enclosing the property on three sides,
a front gate of cast iron tipped with arrowheads?
Does it matter now whether he is young or old?
Does he know himself about any of these things,
on a night like this, at the moment she emerges
from the spirea's whiteness, as though swum up
through a heavy, pounding surf?

                                        Her shirtwaist
is torn, she is hardened by incessant walking
and wandering, by being out in all weathers,
her breasts and her gaunt body have emerged
androgynous and gleaming, she is aglow now,
dusted with shattered blossom as though prepared
for some elusive ritual, and as she gazes at him
she continues to mutter, to murmur — has in fact
never ceased to speak, to utter strange syllables;
whether she understands the words, he cannot tell.

He waits beside the telescope — the gleaming shaft
poised on its tripod — which earlier he pointed
up into the wealth of stars — earlier, alone,
far from the interference of artificial light,
he had come out, he had set up the equipment,
he carried chalkboard in hand for observations —

he began to search, to locate, to gaze into
the huge glimmering hearth of the night sky —

and only moments ago he had found it, had
checked his coordinates, had seen distinctly —
he had looked up and into, looked out far
toward those myriad outflung arms, that turning,
that vast, still, immeasurable unfolding —

and the visitor, strangely silenced now, begins
to come his way, across the fresh-cut grass —
she approaches, strides toward him unhesitant
and unafraid, reaches to touch the viewing aperture,
already in perfect focus, smiles, and leans down —
fragments of white blossom, living particles
of sundered veil cling to her long hair, drip
from her forearms, her rough hands — she sees,
she looks for a long time. There is no sound
except her slight breathing.
                              Finally she begins,
she raises her head, the light is in her eyes,
the shining, and she speaks what comes. He bows
as though in prayer, knowing there is no difference —
it is the far galaxy, great orb and afterimage
in his brain, it is the milk-white hedge cresting
all around them, it is the unsummoned presence
come at last, and always, up through the waves,
it is the voice speaking through all, to all,
here, now, in the darkness, in the starlight.

Beiderbecke Sequence

One / In a Mist

Those quiet moments, after the last number,
when the gig was over, and we loaded up
the cases and the stands, like so much lumber,
and worked to lash the bass drum up on top —
times when it was almost dawn, and colder
at the lake's edge — and those of us who smoked
would light up, waiting, with hunched shoulders,
on the boardwalk — and some would make jokes
about how little we'd earned, and where on earth
we'd go next, and what a life it was. Others
would say nothing, or would stand and gaze
across the lake. It might be the clouds, first,
and then the tree-tops that would gleam and hover
with light, in the fading mist. In the new day.

Two / Flashes

Heading west again, out there somewhere
in Illinois, our makeshift family
would sleep. The driver could reach out through air
tinged with the river's breath. Sometimes you'd see,
in front of you, this truck transporting oil
out to the farms, that had a length of chain
suspended from the axle, rigged to foil
excess electric charge, or so they claimed.
And once, at dusk, when he woke up, and saw
the trail of random sparks, like jackstones thrown
across the road, he asked if we could stay
behind. That glancing rhythm seemed to awe
him into silence. Though we might have known
it would flash out again, next time he played.

Three / Candlelights

After he died, they shipped his body back
to Davenport. His parents tried to right
old wrongs. They staged a service that would lack
for nothing, with sopranos, candlelight,
and Presbyterians praying up a storm.
He would have hated having all that fuss
made over him. That night we tied one on
in some speakeasy — just the three of us
who made the trip. We needed alcohol
to wash away our sins — for having failed
to see it coming, I suppose. We drank
in tribute to his ghost, and toasted all
the times he made those perfect notes prevail.
And gave, for having heard that sound, our thanks.

Four / In the Dark

Years later, I ran into her — someone
he'd known back in those days. Chicago,
maybe, or Des Moines. She had been fun,
and he had liked the way she laughed. The tempo
slowed occasionally; they'd steal away
and find a cottage by some northern lake.
He never took his horn along; he'd say
he'd rather listen to the waves. She'd wake
at night, and hear him sitting in the dark
before an upright he would rent, in case
the urge came over him. At times the sound
was like the wind, at others like the mark
it leaves upon the water. Like the waves,
she said, that he had reached for, and had found.

Jesus Walking on the Water

The final night of the revival a great success!
Ten souls saved for the Lord! Twenty dollars
in the collection plate!
                              And yet this was not
the miracle she had promised, when she wrote,
telling about her missionary days in China,
promising she still had the true gospel fervor,
claiming her preaching would pack the tent;
nor was it the cardboard suitcase she opened,
while the deacons were stacking the chairs
and rolling the tent flaps down for rain,
and putting out the lanterns —
                              the suitcase
out of which she took a jade-green scarf
for Rosalie, and wound it around her neck,
calling her "Sister"; nor the lacquered box
she brought out to show to Emily and Tom,
containing a small glass dome, within which
a miniature orchestra waited for the tap
of the conductor's baton, and each musician
was a dried brown beetle holding a flute
or a violin made of mother-of-pearl.
                              No,
nor her praise for the virtues of living
out here in the country, as they counted
the money, and he gave her exactly half —
as promised in his letter —
                              nor the sound
of wind riffling through the tent, after
all the others were gone, after Rosalie
had taken the children on up the path,
and the last deacon had said good night,

and there was only one coal-oil lantern
hanging from the center pole, and somehow
the wind made it flicker just as he turned
to look at her, and heard the first drops
of rain pelting across the tent —

                              and saw
that her face was neither old nor young,
and continued to see that look in her eyes
even in the darkness that came over them
when he knew exactly what was happening,
at last, on the last night of the revival,
there on the platform, beneath the banner,
next to the lectern —

                              he knew that rain
had finally loosened its fresh, cool smell,
that thunder and lightning had come down
from the far ridge, that he was hearing words
and phrases he could not believe, fragments
of Mandarin and Portuguese, that her voice
caressed certain parts of him even before
her hands and lips began to explore them,
to call from places deep within his body
hot filaments of desire, each strand forced
and drawn out through jeweled apertures —

all this she did patiently, explaining each
touch as she performed it, while in flashes
of lightning that filled the tent he made out
her face, the outline of her hair, her body —
her voice stronger now above the drumming
of the rain as she moved him onto his back
and began to tell him of ways, of secrets
known to courtesans of the ancient palace,
exotic positions never before experienced
by modern man, that gave ungodly pleasure —

and began to demonstrate, slowly, firmly,
this time without telling him the name
of the technique, that strenuous position
called "Wailing Monkey Clasping a Tree,"
until he began to beg, to call out to her,
until he began not to care any longer,
until he began to approach the unbearable,
until the last vestige of doubt had left him,
until it seemed as though mists were rising,
until he began to open, to break into petals
of the flower she kept pressing against him —

until he could grasp without understanding
how she had kept to her promise — soaring
high above him, leaning down at exactly
the right moment and sticking her tongue
in his ear, whispering, laughing softly,
reminding him of the text of the sermon
he had preached earlier that evening —
not simply announcing that miracle now,
but becoming it, showing it to be true.

Glass Negatives

They were my grandfather's. I read about
professors from the college coming late,
to find the crates were gone already, hauled
away for landfill. Given the deep six
beneath some supermarket parking lot,
some cut-rate video store. It made the news
when I lived up near Lauderdale. And yes,
I'll have a drink, I thought you'd never ask.
The waitress knows my call — one-fifty-one.
Well, that old man, he was my grandfather
for sure; but more than that . . . there's something else
that you should know.
                  He was an atheist,
you understand? Back in that little town.
He didn't give a damn for God, and said so,
every chance he got. He was the scourge,
the socialist, the troublemaker, all
the other things they didn't like, rolled
into one. If you grew up in any sort
of place that's off the beaten track, you know
the score. Each town, each neighborhood must have
some misfits in the cast, or else the drama
can't be acted properly. You need
oddballs to make it work. Agnostics, drunks,
poets and prostitutes — without that bunch
to boo and hiss, how would the decent folk
know when to clap? How could they recognize
their starring roles? That was his genius — how
he kept them all in line.
                Behind the scenes,
witness and mirror, never in the picture,
he earned a living showing them themselves —
their first communions, beauty-pageant queens,

73

their teen-age proms and graduation days,
their cornerstones and ceremonial rites.
Kept to himself, and didn't say much, all
those years — a silent, solitary man
who never entered in, or volunteered,
yet never walked away from any fight.
When Wilson got the country into war
he made a sign and marched past city hall
while people threw old shoes and rotten eggs.
They put him into jail for seven days —
for his own good, they said. No trial, no bail,
just locked him up, then couldn't find the key.
It helped with the recruiting, they explained.
He didn't care. It was the principle
that mattered, not what others thought or said.

Back when my mother was a little girl
and prayers were said at school, he made her stand
off in the cloakroom by herself. She cried,
and almost died of shame, and everyone
in town said he was crazy. In a place
like that, where all the chickens do their best
to peck at all the others, any bird
who won't join in is worse than those who do.
You're taught to scorn that sort of person — yet,
there's always some old-timer who will shake
his head, some granny who reminds you that
without a pinch of salt, the bread won't rise.

Most of that stuff took place before my day.
But there was one thing I remember still,
when I was small, that no one talked about.
I was a little girl. Back in Depression times,
when we were living in that house, some nights
my older sister took me by the hand
and we would climb across the bedroom sill
onto a level roof above a porch.

From there, we climbed up to another roof
and then looked through the window of a loft
granddad had rigged up as a studio,
and we could watch, completely unobserved,
on certain nights when he set up his gear
to photograph young women from the town —
and every one without a stitch of clothes.

You have to understand about those days:
we had no air-conditioning back then,
the attic rooms of those old houses stayed
incredibly hot, or cold, except a week
or two in June, right after school got out,
and then again in fall, in late September.
Most of the year, you never went up there
except to bring down something packed away.
But still there came a time of perfect nights,
when our catalpa trees were all in bloom,
and the moon rose, full and bright, shining
across our double bed.
                      We waited there,
until we knew the time had come to start
the climb; we never seemed to be afraid
of falling. When we crouched down, outside
the makeshift studio, we both could see
a room with four bare walls, a pair of lights
bounced off the ceiling, his old four-by-five,
and still another dark-eyed high-school girl
entirely naked, on a rug, or stool.
He would be hidden there beneath his cape,
making adjustments, hardly ever saying
a word. That this took place each spring and fall
was known by every pretty girl in town —
was common knowledge, had been going on
for years. Yet no one ever said a thing
nor did he ever seem to make a print.
The negatives — glass negatives, like all

75

of his best work — were not kept in his store
downtown.
            The two of us would crane and peer
between the cracks of newspapers taped up
against the lower windows. It was clear:
he never touched them, never made advances.
They shifted, took up different poses now
and then, but didn't act lascivious.
In those days people still believed in art —
or what they thought was art, if that would mean
that they were beautiful. He promised them
the lens could see that beauty, could reveal
the truth within, make them immortal. Sure,
and when you're young, you'll live forever, too.

I think they got suspicious when he failed
to give them any prints; they may have thought
the camera had no film. But who would hear
if they complained? Their parents? Teachers?
Minister? They couldn't spill the beans.
Because no prints got out, no one recalled
the earlier times, or made a fuss. Each year
new girls were ready to believe in art
and beauty — and to take it off.
                                My folks
knew all about it, but seemed not to care.
My sister and I took years to understand;
we never talked about what we had seen.
The girls? I can't remember now — we seldom
knew their names. Compared to us, they were
much older — ten or fifteen years, at least.
I couldn't say where they might be; I'd guess
a few have died or disappeared, the rest
have moved away. There might be one or two
still living there, but they would all be old,
with different, married names, and hard to find.
And even if you did, what would they say?
It happened long ago.

I can't remember,
either, how their faces looked, or which
were tall or short, which were true blondes,
or which were bleached. In time they all became
for us — and probably for him — mere volume,
texture, plane, degree of light and shade.
What I remember most from looking in
were all the shadows thrown up by those lights
against the blank walls of that room, across
the curtain and the ceiling. Gradually
the girls' bodies seemed to open up,
to float, like something in a dream — the elbow
poised in space, the flowing hair, the hand
projected into emptiness. The parts
were mortal, but within the first half hour
that was forgotten.
                                    Each model underwent
a kind of change with each new pose, expanding
into something separate and detached,
released into the void — as though she were
alone, and gradually coming into focus
for the first time in her life, discovering
who and what she was, why she had come there,
even though she could not see — had trusted
seeing to him, agreed to stand revealed,
becoming something she had never been
before — and never would be again.
                                                    While
he arranged the spots and changed the lens,
I swear a few of them became transparent —
ethereal, even — essence bared and yet
projected up and out — the whole room filled
with light and flesh and shadowy form, all
intermingled, all become as one.
We saw it happen, yet we had no name
for what we saw, night after night.

                              Who knows?
It's possible he focused on a world
beyond the physical, that he developed
settings, combinations unavailable
to most photographers. But did he really
load the camera? And did he even aim
for something that would show up on the glass?
When I look back, I think it must have been
pure insubstantiality he sought,
rather than shape of thigh, or calf, or curve
of spine. He was that kind of person. Since
by day he had to shoot the commonplace,
the dull, maybe at night, within that room,
he found a way of looking into things,
or through them, rather than straight ahead.
In any case, it doesn't matter now.
We'll never really know.
                              The paper said
it took a workman from the neighborhood
more than an hour to bring those boxes down
three flights of stairs. And no one thought
to hold a single plate up to the light,
to see what might be there. Instead, a calm
and thoroughly efficient mood prevailed:
clear out this worthless stuff, take all that junk
straight to the dump, tear down the house. Sure,
I'll have another one, why not?
                              It's strange,
you figured out a way to find me, here
in this forsaken place. I stop by only
now and then. But still, the light is dim,
and soft, and at my age, a woman needs
the extra help. What did you say, hon?
Why no, that never crossed our minds, I think,
or his. Of course, he shot the two of us
as tiny children, and as little girls
in pinafores, with ribbons in our hair,

and shiny patent-leather shoes with straps,
on Easter morning, and at Christmas, too.
But by the time I'd filled out, grown a curve
or two, and had a figure — he was gone,
forgotten, dead. Not even buried there,
as things turned out. You hadn't heard? It's true,
I swear to god, and had he known about it,
nothing would have pleased him more.

Those towns

are old, those cemeteries started up
a hundred years ago, they had all kinds
of fool restrictions meant to keep out all
the undesirables — free-thinkers, blacks
especially, to this very day, but also
gays, and anybody else they knew
could not be trusted. After he died, the few
who always hated him, whose jealousy
was so intense it reached beyond the grave —
they went to court, and fixed it so my dad
was left no other choice. He went upstate
and bought a single plot. Didn't you know?
That's why he's buried there — as far away
from them in death as he had been in life.
But I digress.

A moment ago, you asked
a curious thing: had I been slightly older,
had the time been right, would I have posed
for him, like all the other girls? It's strange,
but all these years, I never asked myself
that question. Both of us were too involved
with what went on. He knew that we were there,
outside the window, looking in. We were
a kind of audience *in absentia*,
hidden away — our very presence proof
of what it takes to make light possible,
that gives contrast and definition, even
reveals what's there. You have to realize

79

that we were kids, just nine or ten years old,
at most. We had no words for what we saw,
no way of grasping. We were innocence
and vision, both at once. It might have been
a window onto Eden we gazed through
each time we watched.   And all this talk about
exposure, light and shade, and camera angles,
everything I've told you — all that came
much later, after I had grown up, left
that little town behind, gone out into
the world, and traveled, changed, become
whatever it is I am today, the woman
you find me now — a castaway, perhaps,
sitting in this bar, listening to the waves.

But does it really matter? Even buried
beneath that parking lot, that burger joint,
that strip mall at the edge of town, even
broken into fragments that can never
be assembled again, even ground to dust —
what she and I were seeing, what he knew
we could not help but see, outside the room
but peering in — was something far beyond
appearances, beyond the visible.
And that was what he was chose to let us see.
I think he wanted us to see it, if we could.

That was the offer made to all those girls,
that was what led the braver ones to come
to the back stairs, late at night, through air
turned cool and lush, and full of fragrance,
with peepers throbbing in the maple trees —
that was why they came, why they took off
all their clothes, and stood there in the light.
Step out of yourself even once — you'll find
it can't be taken back — it's done forever.

And now? Based on the handful of old prints
you've run to ground — glassblowers hard at work,
wheat harvesters, the one with Mother Jones
and Debs and Big Bill Haywood arm in arm —
you claim America has never been shown
so clear, so pure, so honestly. And now
the exhibitions, lectures, dissertations
tantalize: he might have been the peer
of Walker Evans, or that woman named Lange.
The best collectors own his work; if more
turned up, the gold rush would be on.
                                    You're smart.
You tracked me down, bought me a drink or two,
and hoped I'd say the magic words — if not
a cache of unknown prints, at least some clue,
some other place to look. I'm sorry, hon,
I've told you all I know. They're gone. That's all.
I didn't save a one. I kept a few
when I was young. But you know how it is:
you're busy raising kids, and getting by,
and things like that begin to disappear
once you have reached a certain age.
                                    You're left
with nothing more than memories of light
and shade, and long ago. The road ends here,
the continent, too. Even the sea becomes,
in time, a world of pure forgetfulness.
Close your eyes now, and listen to the waves.

Picking Stone

Speak your latent conviction, and it shall be the universal
sense; for the inmost in due time becomes the outmost. We
recognize our own rejected thoughts: they come back to us
with a certain alienated majesty.

Emerson, "Self-Reliance"

One

Up north, along the east shore of the lake,
they grow apples, and all kinds of cherries.
Each spring, when the men go out to plow
for asparagus or corn, they find rocks
that had not been there before, boulders
worked up from the earth during the winter,
a harsh crop of stone rising in the furrows.

Two

On spring evenings farmers lead their families
past the bare, twisted trees, to go pick stone
while the light is still good. They spread out
across the fresh-turned earth, following
a flatbed truck, searching with their hands
through the broken clods, grasping, struggling,
helping each other heave up what they find.

Three

The two older boys, still in baseball uniforms
from a game at the Legion, take turns driving.
Each fills the pockets of his windbreaker
with bits of worked stone — points, scrapers,
tools that have lain underground all this time —
that their grandfather taught them to recognize.
They keep them in cigar boxes under the bed

Four

and seldom take them out anymore. Now,
they give the best stones to the smaller sister,
who walks with the old man, who wants to do
what he says, follow where he goes. The father
moves back and forth, now down on his knees
with a son, brushing sand from a boulder,
deciding they will come back and get it

Five

with the tractor, now carrying the baby
for a while, suddenly handing it to his wife
and going to help the oldest daughter, who
has lifted a rock and hugs it to her body,
staggering, as though she were burdened
with grief. While he works, while he moves
from one group to another, he looks beyond

Six

the trees, across the land's swell, at the lake,
that is vast and unblemished and still,
gleaming with evening light. All winter
it has waited like a great slab of granite,
giving off its hoarded warmth to the land
at the lake's edge, to the roots and the sap
waiting beneath the snow. Now the lake

Seven

is cold, and will stay that way till summer.
Thunderheads will come from the west,
snapping off branches, bringing the warmth.
At night, if he were not too tired to dream,
the farmer would see the lake, know it to be
the same stone he has lifted all these years,
that he cannot put down, nor hand to another.

Eight

Hurrying along, he senses that a storm
is gathering north of Old Mission point.
His daughter, who dropped to her knees
when he tried to help her, who let the stone
roll away, who walks now, angry, alone,
across the rows with the wind in her hair —
his daughter knows when they have a load

Nine

the two boys will drive it south of the barn
and dump it against the pile. That is what
bewilders her: the craggy pile of rocks
at the far end of the barnyard, where she
and her brothers have climbed and played,
that has always been there. Though they add
new rocks each spring, it never seems to change,

Ten

growing neither smaller nor larger. It is
the mountain that holds her back, balanced
against her dream of leaving the home-place.
Now that she is older, she hates the stones,
hates being taken out to pick them, believes
that whatever weight she adds to the pile
falls through the earth, creeps underground,

Eleven

rises again, to wear the skin from her fingers.
The grandfather holds her little sister's hand,
he is telling the same story, only this time
it is grandmother who is the stone now.
She is under the earth, she will come back,
she will be unchanged. He walks on, silent.
He lifts nothing now. The land and the lake

Twelve

he once held so close their shadows fell
between his own body and hers, as they slept —
that weight has been handed over. Now it is
no heavier than clouds on the horizon, gulls,
wind in the dry grass. Sometimes he thinks
he can hear the older girl slip from the house,
go to meet someone near the pile of stones,

Thirteen

steal off to find some place out of the wind.
At other times it's the sound of the wind,
or the memory of being in the barn, years ago,
with the girl from the next farm. He thinks
he knows why his granddaughter lifts stones
as though to hurt something inside herself,
unable to accept the dream of things that grow

Fourteen

and move about in darkness, and return.
He alone sees how the stones they gather —
straining to fling them into the truck bed —
begin to fade in the last light, changing
to slate, to the lost colors of the lake
before the rain finally sweeps across it.
By nightfall, his sleep will be all these things

Fifteen

dreamed together: currents of water and stone,
a rising and a falling. The father calls out
through the sudden wind, they must gather
a full load before going back. They bend
to the earth, searching. The mother turns
to help the sons, who pry with an iron bar
against a great gray rock. They will not quit,

Sixteen

they begin to roar as they bear down on it.
Bits of broken stone fall from their pockets,
and the daughter, leaving the smallest child
in the middle of a row, bends to retrieve them.
A curtain of rain sweeps through the far trees.
The baby, left alone, as though distinguishing
dream from darkness, rises to go toward it.

Shelterbelt

There is no single reality. . . . you nevertheless go on,
walking towards utopia, which may not exist, on a bridge
which might end before you reach the other side.

Marguerite Young, interview
Review of Contemporary Fiction

Again, on the third night, they landed in the trees
west of the house, and she dressed and went out
to have a look — and saw them against thin clouds
and stars and the glint of a new moon. They kept
gathering and re-gathering, tossing and turning,
like the lightest of sleepers, as though searching
for some part of a dream that had drifted away,
its memory beyond them.
                         Each year they returned,
usually a few days before the solstice, pausing
in their quest, stopping for a night or two. Crows,
come from the bottomland — thousands of them
bent on roosting in one particular tree, rising up
at the slightest noise or distraction, wheeling about
in one great unfolding wave, then collapsing,
filling the leafless tree again, settling down,
brooding in some lost, indecipherable language,
waiting for the next alarm, or sudden ascension.

She had watched their arrivals since childhood,
when an aunt or grandfather would bundle her up
and take her out on the porch, and point to them,
and recall some old tale about what it all meant.
The crows were choosing a new leader, perhaps,
or they had lost their way, and had stopped to ask
if anyone remembered.

"But there are so many!"
she would exclaim, while they surged and circled
above the house, caught up in their slow cycle
of rising and falling. In a few minutes' time
they would settle again among the gaunt limbs
and branches, fussing and finally growing still,
like elders dozing off during church.
                                        The old man
would clap his hands together, again and again,
and out from the tree, in all directions, the birds
would explode in a cacophony of shrieking,
a buffeting of wings.
                        It had been no different
this year. They had chosen a red oak, sprung up
in the shelterbelt of coniferous trees, planted
by that same grandfather, before she was born.
She remembered this tree. During reunions,
in the long-ago summers, the visiting cousins
who were big enough to reach its lowest limbs,
would hoist themselves up, and find perches,
and sit there talking and laughing.
                                        Below,
around the base of this tree, the smaller children
would gather, and begin to weep, and wish aloud
that they were big enough to reach the limbs,
and sit there with the others. "Don't worry,"
word came to them, "someday you'll be tall,
you'll be able to get up here on your own."
Then the older cousins would climb down,
and take up the smaller children, one by one,
and set them on the limbs, steadying them,
as though they had all come to the carnival,
on a summer evening, in the sawdust ring
where shaggy brown ponies walk in circles,
and each child had been lifted up and placed,
for the first time, on a pony's back, and told
to hold fast to the leather pommel.

This year,
the first night she heard them above the house,
she sensed the rhythms too irregular to follow,
and the sporadic calling, the troubled croaking.
It was all familiar, as though from somewhere,
out of the cold night, someone or something
had begun to speak.

A phrase from an old hymn,
perhaps, or a scrap of verse, a humorous line
recited aloud at a school picnic. There was, too,
in that slow torrent, the sound of working men
calling through the snow or the fog, talking
to the animals, comforting them, assuring them.
And there was a hint of women's voices, too,
young and old, sharing the tasks of fall canning,
snapping green beans while the Mason jars
rattle and jingle in the cookers on the stove.

This speech came to her in shreds and patches,
the sounds broken and tinny, but she knew it,
heard it somewhere in the crows' colloquy,
recognized it welling up from some far place,
until their harsh language rolled back again,
washing over everything.

She was at the beach,
in the sunlight, watching the waves smooth down
the letters she had drawn with a stick in the sand,
the waves taking away what she had written there,
that had lasted only a moment.

When she was older,
in the fifth or sixth grade, in the middle of a lesson,
she had run from the classroom, and hurried out
to stand by the fence, near the row of hollyhocks.
The teacher had left her there until recess, then
gone to find her. The lesson had been about nouns
for collections of things. One example given was

"a murder of crows." According to an old folk tale,
the crows assembled to form tribunals — to judge,
at times to punish, an errant member of the flock.
If the verdict went against the defendant, the bird
was killed.

But her grandfather never told her that,
nor her aunts, and with their help she had made up
her own account of the reason for their gathering.
They were enchanted creatures, on a long journey
to a place they did not know, but only dreamed of,
and their deliberations, on cold winter evenings,
their restlessness — all this was a way of exchanging
bits and pieces of what each recalled of the dream.
When they remembered, and sensed the direction
in which they should go, to reach this fabulous place,
they rose up a final time and flew across the fields,
and did not return until the following year.

True:
they always seemed to lose their way. But each year
they came back, and kept searching, still believing
in a place that was always beckoning.

She recalled
holding on to the wire fence, trying to quiet
her sobbing by reciting this story aloud, feeling
the tears running down her cheeks, noticing
honeybees drifting among the hollyhock blossoms.
The recess bell rang. Soon the teacher was there,
to put a cool, damp cloth to her face.

Now, the crows,
barely murmuring, muffled and still, settled down
in the limbs of the tree. This third night of their visit
had comforted her. She felt as though a worn quilt
had been drawn over her — an old coverlet made
of a thousand fragments, with a multitude of stitches
carefully sewn. The birds had returned, as before,
and they seemed to give witness — at times their calls

almost made sense, but soon dispersed into a cloud
of uncertainty and a whirlwind of bodies, restless
and searching.
    But there was something else, too,
something new, and when on this third night, after
she had gazed up at them long enough, and sensed
their indifference to her presence, she came inside,
and returned to her bed, and switched off the light,
and lay there surrendering to this new dimension,
one she had not noticed before, over the years.
She could hear the shuttered sound of their wings,
folding and unfolding, in no unison at all, out
of synch with their cries, but forming a backdrop
of sound, against which the wind itself, sifting
through the wall of evergreens, seemed distant,
and not to matter, and was lost in the soughing
and sighing of their bodies in motion.
           Even this
she remembered now, recalling the odd delight
of taking the visiting cousins out to the hen house,
while the grown-ups stayed in the kitchen to talk,
or sat on the front porch, churning the ice-cream.
The hen house, with its bank of dusty windows
facing south, its closeness, its pungency —
              the door
scraping the sill, and the stir of wings whirring
and stretching, the feathered necks shivering,
over and over, among those shadows, as though
dozens of wicker baskets were being opened
and closed, in some long and patient succession —
some elemental response that meant nothing
and went nowhere, a sound as old and enveloping
as the darkness itself.
        It was their wings, now —
the crows' wings, in their sporadic circling flights
above the shelterbelt, and the punctuation of silence

when they finally became still, and settled down
for a moment or two. The rush of those wings
become a fabric against which everything else
finds a place, at last —

              like sleep, and the way
you surrender to its texture. Or children, weeping
at the foot of a green tree, longing to be lifted
into a world they can barely imagine.

                    Or birds,
circling through a cold and unforgiving night,
searching for something they will never find,
some dimension that draws them on —

                  a dream
they encountered once, and might locate again,
should they endure, and persist in their journey.

The Bones

They are a most ancient instrument. In a time long ago, I heard them —
a sound that will probably die out, and not be heard again, now that
the Twentieth Century is over. If I could, I would describe it for you —

but it is wordless, and entirely evocative, and can only be demonstrated.
Yet I remember it well, since back in the '70s and '80s, on afternoons
in the summer, I used to get together with a man named William Johnson,

who was born in East Texas in 1905, and who, when still a small boy,
had been taught to play the bones by his grandfather, who had been a slave,
and a master of many instruments, including the bones. The secret

of playing the bones is all in the wrists, and has little to do with the fingers,
as William Johnson would occasionally point out. They were not bones,
either, but matching pairs of hard, molded plastic sticks he had purchased

for two dollars, in a music store in the Loop, in 1936. Held a certain way
between the fingers of each hand, and "snaggled" back and forth to the music,
they made a sound *like a cold wind blowing through the canebrake,*

or a freight train, on a winter night, passing over the trestle bridge.
Sometimes I could almost feel *the rise and fall of the ties, the wheels
clicking, the patient creaking of the boxcars.*   In the Johnsons' front parlor

stood an ebony-cased Chute & Butler upright piano, built in 1898,
and sometimes on summer afternoons we would play Joplin together,
or Scott, or Lamb, or Artie Matthews — all of those lost, stately compositions

dating from before the First War, before Victrolas and player pianos,
when the only music you could hear was the music made in your presence.
Some say ragtime is intensely lyrical, that it serves as a cultural bridge

back to the melodies and tunes of the Civil War — to the foursquare marches
and the dented bugles and tarnished silver cornets that spread across
the country, after that war, into the villages and hamlets of Missouri

and Illinois, and up along the Ohio River. Others say it is percussive,
and African in nature, and that when it slid over to the piano bench
in railroad towns like Sedalia, and in riverfront towns like St. Louis,

it set up rhythms that had been lost and forgotten, or dispersed
to the fields and the bottomlands, but were gathered up again
and given new life — sounds that would continue to flow and merge

with other kinds of music that were to follow, and help to define the century.
Lyric, percussive. . . the terms do not matter, for certainly it is both,
and that is the way William Johnson played the bones, hunched over

on a straight chair next to the piano, concentrating on the rhythms
and ratcheting patterns of sound he produced with them. With a nod,
I would begin to glide through the pastel rooms of "Heliotrope Bouquet,"

or hover beneath the marquee of "Topliner," or the downpour of "Climax Rag"—
*music box on a dresser, in a darkened hotel room, brass key revolving
in time with the blades of an overhead fan. . . .* You might well object

that no one plays this kind of music anymore, those days are forgotten,
we are far more progressive and modern. But such were the pastimes,
once, in the late afternoons and evenings, when people came together

not only for the pleasure of hearing music, but also for the delight
of making it — for it was something to be held in common, *and passed on,
coaxing it until it flowed out through the windows and along the porch,*

and onto the street, into the fields. As I remember, it was not a long walk
to the house where the Johnsons lived. Down the hill, over the creek,
across the double tracks of the old Bee Line, past a stretch of storefronts

made of red brick, boarded up now and abandoned. Then the path
beneath the Interstate, with all the cars and trucks roaring overhead,
and out into the sunlight again, and a field of red clover. Their house

was the only one left standing, at the edge of that field. Katherine,
my friend's wife, might be out in the back yard, hanging up the wash.
Sometimes, after we got underway, she would come into the parlor

and sing along with us, in her clear alto voice — adding neither words
nor melody but something evoked by the moment, part invention
and part response to the intricate motion of her husband's hands, part

an echo of what I was finding among the keys. *Along the stairways
and the dusty landings, among barrels and packing crates, the old sounds,
waiting to be brought back.* . . . When we had finished, when we had made

enough music for a while, William Johnson would put the bones away,
in their original cardboard box, and I would collect my sheet music,
and make a bundle of it, to carry home again. Katherine would bring in

glasses of iced tea for us to drink, and the three of us would sit together
on the side porch, in the cool of a summer evening. Sometimes
they would talk about this country, and how it had seemed to them

when they were young — Texarkana to St. Louis, Memphis to Chicago,
Milwaukee and Dayton — and the orchestras they had heard, the theaters,
the places they had worked, their visits to Liberia, the music they had made

and shared, all of their lives. *Call and response, Sunday morning solo . . .
shaken tambourine, diamondback whirring of the bones . . . shadows
cast by the blades of the overhead fan.* . . . The two of them are gone now,

and the house is gone, too, and even that long century has come to an end.
But the freight trains still make their runs in the night, and the rails still rock
back and forth, beneath the wheels, and sometimes I find myself waking

to that clicking sound, and I imagine that it is the shake of the bones I hear,
and the voices calling — *Come now, in the early evening, let us bring back
those forgotten strains. Yes, yes,* I want to reply, *let us make that old music again.*

Lost Bridge

One

They said there was nothing left at all, after the rising and falling
       of the water level, over twenty summers and winters.
But I still wanted to go back, that November day, along the old road,
       dropping down through those same hills, the valley up ahead

coming into view, stripped clean of everything now, a vast slope
       of mud — and the lake itself, at the bottom, motionless
in the bleak light, giving off no reflection. Parked at the road's end
       was a brown panel truck with a state seal on the door.

A man in a uniform stood drawing a net through a puddle (a tire rut,
       really), lifting up fish stranded by the annual lowering.
He counted each catch into a plastic bucket. Mostly small fry —
       bluegill, from the look of them, and a few sunnies.

Each time, he wrote something on a clipboard. I watched him fling
       bucket after bucket of fingerlings out across the mud
where they flopped around and finally grew still. I walked farther
       along the edge and saw water in dozens of pockets

and shallows, and in each of them something still stirred,
       drifting back and forth. A hundred yards beyond,
where the Mississinewa once flowed beneath the covered bridge,
       the winter pool lay like a great black stone.

Two

When the officer drove away in his truck, I had it all to myself.
       I took out the map the old farmer had sketched for me,
the night before, in the hospital room, and set out to find
       the peninsula where the Lost Bridge Cemetery had been.

"You'll see, you'll see," he told me, between gasps for breath;
         he fussed with the plastic tube fitted into his nose,
then fell back against the pillow. I would see something, he promised,
         that was starting to come up, where there was nothing —

something working its way through the darkness loosed over the valley,
         rising toward the light, summoned by that long watering;
a strange crop, that had waited all these years to come forth,
         and could neither be harvested now, nor made to flower.

There were signs everywhere warning me to keep out. Lost Bridge
         had been a few campsites down-river, beneath a steep bluff.
The fishing was good, and cabins and cottages followed. A dance-hall
         stood out over the water, next to a dock where bootleggers

tied up their boats; people congregated there on Saturday nights.
         The Grange shut down in the '30s, the schoolhouse
in the '50s. After the reservoir came, nothing was left except
         the bluff itself, almost an island now, unreachable,

fenced off, posted. Studying his map, I picked up a stretch
         of the old road, followed it to the marshy edge, and waded
a hundred yards of brackish, knee-deep water to the other side.
         The road emerged there, crumbling, eaten by vegetation

but leading up through vines and brambles toward the cemetery
         on the eastern slope, which was underwater eight months
of the year. No one had ventured that way for a long time.
         I worked to get through, breaking and twisting the branches.

Three

"Where the road starts to drop toward the river, take the path
         to the right, and stay with it." Past a small island —
a clump of scrub willow — he had marked the place with a cross.
         Now, it was a level stretch of mud pocked with tree stumps

97

and pools of dying fish. The secret he had found during his rambles,
        and waited to tell me about, was there. I looked out
in disbelief, not comprehending: where nothing should have remained,
        I saw huge blocks and cubes of stone, each larger

than those placed over any grave. Two dozen of them at least,
        no two identical, scattered like a handful of enormous dice
across the slick plain. I went closer. They were featureless
        and smooth, caked with mud left by the receding waters.

Some were half buried, others showed broken edges and corners;
        I scratched at the scale, but could find no inscriptions.
They waited now like pieces from some fallen temple — broken,
        battered fragments, survived beyond all memory of their origin.

Mud sucked and squished beneath my boots as I walked among them,
        trying to understand.   The entire cemetery had been moved
a quarter of a century earlier: all the coffins taken up,
        headstones numbered, everything in the plat-book uprooted

and trucked five miles to the north. I had passed the new site
        coming along that same road, not an hour before. I sat down
on one of the stones and felt its surface: not stone at all,
        but formed concrete, the aggregates bleeding through.

"Working its way up," he had said. "Growing where we thought
        they had taken out everything." Blocks of concrete,
of a size and scale that made no sense in that little town. "Try
        to imagine," he said, grinning at me, "where they came from."

        Four

You would have lived there all your life, except for the time
        you served in the Civil War. You could have bought a place,
but you went, when they called you, and spent fourteen months
        at Vicksburg, on picket, so Ulysses Grant could go out east

98

and whip Bob Lee. You weren't born in this valley, but farther back,
          in another one, east of Wheeling. You came out here
with your father, and when you were old enough to handle a team
          you helped him clear the trees and burn off the stumps.

You were baptized in the Mississinewa. Your wife had five children
          and lost three to diphtheria. You've heard of airplanes
but you've never seen one. You've farmed a hundred and sixty acres;
          you're ready to leave it to your son. Now your wife dies.

Everything takes its time in your world. The river, flowing west
          past the boat landing, never seems to hurry. The second day,
you go to the churchyard with your son, and the two of you
          dig the grave. Later, when everyone's gone, you fill it in.

A week after that, just before noon, while your son is out plowing,
          you go to the church to meet the man from the county seat
and help him unload the granite stones you ordered. Next morning
          you start to dig another hole for the footing. It's warm,

and from up there on the ridge you can look out across the valley:
          all the hardwoods are in leaf, the gardens turning green,
sounds of hammering echo from a new house being built, children
          gather at recess in the schoolyard, singing and playing games.

You dig, and think of the times when you first knew her, back
          when you were courting. What she was like. You keep digging.
Halfway through the morning the hired man pulls up in the wagon,
          sets off the keg of cement you've kept dry in the barn.

He takes the wagon on up to the pit behind Samuelson's farm,
          and shovels sand and gravel into the bed. After dinner,
he's back, and the two of you unload the mortar box and the hoes.
          You begin to mix up the concrete for the footing.

Cement is expensive. It's a big hole. The stonecutter left you
          a tripod and a block and tackle to lift the two stones.
The hired man makes jokes about how nothing's ever going to move
          this marker, not in a thousand years. You keep stirring

and mixing the concrete, shoveling it into the hole. Your son comes
      with half a dozen boulders plowed up in the field.
You drop them onto the surface, one by one, pushing them down
      with a broom-handle, and add more mix on top of them.

While you wait for the footing to set, the hired man rigs up the tripod.
      Together you hoist the plinth-stone into position,
easing it down until it comes to rest on the wet slab. No need
      for connecting rods: nothing will ever shake this day's work.

The next morning the three of you come back to fit the headstone
      and mortar it into place. Your own name is there, too,
and the day of your birth. Five years later your son pays a stonecutter
      to come from town and chisel in the day of your death.

    Five

They did their own work, with their own hands. Fought wars, dug wells
      and ditches, raised barns, helped animals give birth.
Cement was expensive, labor cheap. When it came time to anchor stones
      in the churchyard, they did a good job. But the waters,

moving up and down that slope in ways no one could have anticipated,
      fifty or a hundred years later, kept gnawing away
at what the undertakers left behind. After the plinths and headstones
      were broken off and carried to higher ground, after

the crumbling boxes and powdery containers had been dug up and moved,
      the footings remained — lodged in a soil that had been
handled and sifted many times now, an earth that had begun to drift
      each time the waters returned. Everyone in that world

knows how stones surface each spring, beckoned by the plow's tongue —
      summoned by the freeze and thaw, some said — or drawn up
by the waxing moon — a seasonal tide that brings forth arrowheads
      and stone tools, after the rains, scattering them among

the furrows, year after year, more reliably than any grain or leaf.
        No farmhouse lacks its cigar box of points and scrapers
offered up spontaneously by the earth. Inevitably this process, too,
        this slow uprooting, working hugely, helped resurrect them:

a score of table-sized blocks finding their way toward the light,
        sprouting up from that harsh, abandoned field — memorials
useless and bare, that had risen in response to deep rhythms,
        and could neither be harvested now, nor made to flower.

    Six

I never saw him again. Relatives moved him to a warmer climate,
        in Southern Pines, North Carolina, where he sat on a side porch
and fed fox squirrels, and set traps for moles. I sent him a packet
        of castor-bean seeds to keep the moles away. He wrote back:

the squirrels wouldn't touch them. Two years later his niece forwarded
        a letter meant for me, started just before his last stroke.
She had run across it in a desk drawer. Stapled to it was a clipping
        I still carry in my billfold, a four-line filler about moles:

"To perform work equal to that of the average mole,
        a man would have to excavate, in a single night,
a tunnel wide enough to easily permit the passage of his own body;
        such a tunnel would be thirty-seven miles long."

"Received parts four and five of your poem," the letter began.
        "You couldn't have been farther off base. Nobody would dig
holes like that if they didn't have to. All those old farmers
        up in that township were tighter than the bark on a tree.

"There's not a one of them would have spent a nickel on cement
        if he could have figured out some other way of doing it.
Those weren't footings. That wasn't the churchyard, either,
        it was a quarter mile on up the road, and a left turn,

"not a right. You didn't think very much about what you saw.
        Back when they were getting ready to build that dam,
the Corps of Engineers sent a full-bird colonel out to tell us
        how it would help control all the flooding downstream.

"They called a meeting in the old schoolhouse. Everybody was there
        and everybody was fit to be tied. Clayton Sample stood up
and told how he read in *Life* magazine about another dam
        the Army built out west that silted up in twenty years

"and the flooding went right on. So why bother building this one
        in the first place, and kicking everybody off their land?
But it didn't make any difference what we thought, they went
        right ahead and did what they wanted. When that happened

"we all decided they just didn't care, that sometimes that's how
        big government works. But solid concrete doesn't float;
you should have learned that while you were out there fooling around
        at that fancy eastern university. Those weren't footings

"you saw scattered across that mud flat. When Sefe Graybill's crew
        was moving the old pioneer graves out of Monument City
and Maple Grove and all those other little towns, somebody else
        was moving something in. Something the Feds didn't want

"anybody to know about. Concrete won't float unless it's hollow,
        unless it's some kind of container with something inside it,
something they're ashamed of — sealed up in a hurry and dropped off
        in a place that's never going to see daylight again, according

"to their initial calculations. Did you ever wonder why the bankers
        and lawyers never got around to building any summer homes
on that reservoir? Use your head. If the Grecian urn had glowed
        in the dark, would Keats — " The letter breaks off here.

Seven

It's still a nice place to go on summer afternoons. There are
            boat-launching ramps, with picnic areas, spaced along
the south shore. No swimming. No condominiums. I never bothered
            to go back to Lost Bridge, to see if they're still there.

I know they're gone. Buried in some other place, hidden from sight.
            It's pleasant to drive up there and park in one of the lots
and find a picnic table, and sit and look out at all the boats
            cris-crossing the water. Most of them are pulling skiers;

the fishermen get up early, and head for the coves, before the crowds
            start to arrive. I go sit there sometimes and think about
conversations we had, on days like that, looking out, back before
            he stumbled across the containers at Lost Bridge.

"Swamps," he said once, trying to re-light his pipe in the wind.
            "Wetlands. That's what we didn't realize — Clayton and Sefe
and Agnes and everybody else who lived in that little town,
            or nearby. You don't have floods if you don't have rain

running off the land every five minutes, and into the creeks, then
            on down the drain. You don't have floods if you got beavers.
Used to be a lot of dams along these rivers. The ground was soggy,
            even in the big forests. Spongy. The water stayed there,

it didn't flush straight on down the Mississippi watershed, taking
            half an inch of topsoil every year. We changed all that.
With our axes. With our ditches and tiled fields. Our steel traps.
            We dried it out so finally some bureaucrat from Washington

could come along, a hundred years later, and decide he would
            centralize everything, with a reservoir, and get control."
He snorted, put down his pipe, and threw the last matchstick away.
            "There's no such thing as control. There's only balance."

Eight

No one remembers now why they called it Lost Bridge. No map
        goes back that far. At dawn one October morning, a year ago,
I rowed out through the mists to a point half a mile beyond the bluff
        and watched a hundred sandhill cranes lift from the water

and circle around the island, keeping the trees between us until
        I finally came about. Eventually they settled down again
in the same place they've been stopping for thousands of years
        on their migrations back and forth between the Gulf of Mexico

and Hudson Bay. That particular place, once a river, now a lake
        that waxes and wanes, is still a fulcrum for their journeying,
a balancing point. I began to row back toward the landing, facing
        the ridge where the sun would rise. The lake was so calm

the early morning light spread out over the mist-whitened surface
        in one vast, unbroken gleam. For a moment, beneath the boat,
the water turned clear, to the farthest depth, and I could see
        how I was moving along the original course of the river,

following and yet still not being determined by those twists
        and turns, those long-forgotten shapes and contours.
Nor was there a current carrying me now. Suspended, borne up
        by some invisible stillness, I moved under my own power.

The bluff at Lost Bridge came into view, half of its trees
        and weedy coves still dark with shadow. Slowly, oarlocks
creaking, each dip of the oars trailing swirls in the water,
        I left that world behind, and rowed across the shining lake.

Acknowledgments

The author thanks the editors of the following publications where these poems first appeared:

Raccoon Grove	*Images*
Exhumation	*Edge City Review*
Covered Bridge	*TriQuarterly*
Visit	*New Letters / Sparrow*
Catalpa	*South Dakota Review*
Coxey's Army	*People's Culture*
Mussel Shell	*IndiAnnual*
Reminiscence	*Painted Bride Quarterly*
Spirea	*Iowa Review*
Beiderbecke Sequence	*Iambs & Trochees*
Jesus Walking	*The Scream Online*
Glass Negatives	*Edge City Review*
Picking Stone	*Zone 3*
Shelterbelt	*Raintown Review*
The Bones	*Sou'wester*
Lost Bridge	*Riveries*

"Raccoon Grove" was reprinted in *Under Open Sky: Poets on William Cullen Bryant*. Edited by Norbert Krapf. New York: Fordham University Press, 1986.

"Visit" received the *New Letters* Literary Award for Poetry in 1992. The judge was Philip Levine.

"Picking Stone" received the Rainmaker Award for Poetry from *Zone 3* magazine in 2002. The judge was Marilyn Chin.

About the Author

Jared Carter is a Midwesterner from Indiana. If he were to be granted one wish, he would like to spend a day at the Chicago World's Fair of 1893. Information about his previous books of poetry may be found on his web site at www.jaredcarter.com.

Printed in the United States
58950LVS00005B/483